AMERICA'S
HOLY GROUND

General Sherman, the largest tree in the world by volume, Sequoia National Park

AMERICA'S HOLY GROUND

61 FAITHFUL REFLECTIONS ON OUR NATIONAL PARKS

BRAD LYONS & BRUCE BARKHAUER

chalice press

Saint Louis, Missouri

An imprint of Christian Board of Publication

ChalicePress.com

Print: 9780827200753
EPUB: 9780827200784
EPDF: 9780827200791

Printed in the United States of America

To Beej, Summer, and Zoe, my big-eyed kids who helped me to see the parks through new eyes: may you use this book in your future trips to our national parks, and may those you love accompany you with joy, wonder, and awe for God's creation.

—Brad

To Dan, Alan, Rebekah, Henry, and Teddy: may you enjoy the world with the same delight as the Creator who claimed it was all "very good," and may you exercise your dominion in a way that preserves its legacy and wonder for your children and grandchildren.

—Bruce

Bear tracks, Kobuk Valley National Park

Mountain smoke in autumn, Great Smoky Mountains National Park

CONTENTS

McDonald Lake, Glacier National Park

Blue Hen Falls, Cuyahoga Valley National Park

ACKNOWLEDGMENTS

First and foremost, I am grateful to my parents, Brenda and Stan. Thank you for those first trips to national parks—Carlsbad Caverns, Yellowstone, the Grand Canyon, Black Canyon of the Gunnison, Rocky Mountain and all the other incredible places to which you took us—and for helping to connect those places with what I'd learned in church. (Sorry about all the fighting in the backseat with Stacy, but her stuff really was on my side, by at least half an inch. And thank you, Stacy, for not strangling me when we fought.) Thank you also for helping me to see the beauty in what so many consider to be ordinary places.

Thank you, Courtney, for joyously and energetically rounding out the research that made this project so much fun, even the Cleetwood Trail at Crater Lake.

Thanks especially to my kids, for allowing me to concentrate when I needed time to get work done, but also for being interested in this project and in the world around us, especially when indulging my on-the-fly historical and geographic research.

Thank you, Bruce and Laura, for your hospitality that summer evening in 2015 when the first seeds of this book were planted. That'll teach you to have company over!

Finally, thanks to the staff and board of the Christian Board of Publication and Chalice Press, especially Deborah Arca, Gail Stobaugh, Connie Wang, Chuck Blaisdell, K. J. Reynolds, and Corinne Lattimer, for breathing life into this project and for seeing its opportunities. Thanks also to Vicky Shea for the cover and interior design and to Connie for the beautiful final book. And thank you to the National Park Service and other photographers, whose photos add so much beauty to this book.

—Brad

I am grateful to my parents, who insisted that I "go play outside" and for their willingness to let me explore the world around me. That meant bicycle rides into the Rocky River Reservation on the west side of Cleveland, a hike in the woods or down to Lakewood park to wander along the shores of Lake Erie. We took vacations to fish the lakes of the Madawaska Valley and the Halliburton Highlands of Ontario, Canada. My first places of wonder were not national parks, but they prepared me to experience more fully what our parks have to offer.

I am thankful for the Lilly Foundation and a clergy renewal grant in 2006 that prompted the original idea for this project, and for my friend Brad Lyons, who took this notion and helped craft it into something special. We share a love for the natural world and a passion for the written word, both of which are vehicles for inspiration. Brad's patience and persistence and probing questions have been a blessing. To the board of the Christian Board of Publication: you have given me a gift by allowing me to contribute to this project.

For my wife and partner in life, Laura: thank you for encouraging me and believing in me even when I don't. There are not enough words to express my appreciation for you.

I am also grateful for the many unnamed camp counselors, park rangers, nature guides, interpretive programs, and the lifelong support of the church. Collectively they have given me the tools to integrate science and faith *without* conflict and *with* mutual appreciation for the value of both.

And to you, the reader: thank you for allowing us to share with you some of our thoughts about how beautiful the world is. Let's keep it that way.

—Bruce

Bison crossing the Yellowstone River, Yellowstone National Park

From both of us:

Thank you to those who had the vision to see God's blessings in these sixty-one magnificent places.

Thank you to those who protected them in the past.

Thank you to those who protect and maintain them today.

Thank you to those who will protect them in the future.

And, of course, thanks be to God!

Joshua Tree National Park

INVOCATION

"Blessed be your glorious name, and may it be exalted above all blessing and praise. You alone are the LORD. You made the heavens, even the highest heavens, and all their starry host, the earth and all that is on it, the seas and all that is in them. You give life to everything, and the multitudes of heaven worship you."

—NEHEMIAH 9:5b–6 (NIV)

When I look at your heavens, the work of your fingers,
the moon and the stars that you have established;
what are human beings that you are mindful of them,
mortals that you care for them?
Yet you have made them a little lower than God
and crowned them with glory and honor.
You have given them dominion over the works of your hands;
you have put all things under their feet,
all sheep and oxen,
and also the beasts of the field,
the birds of the air, and the fish of the sea,
whatever passes along the paths of the seas.

—PSALM 8:3–8 (NRSV)

Let the heavens be glad, and let the earth rejoice;
let the sea roar, and all that fills it;
let the field exult, and everything in it.
Then shall all the trees of the forest sing for joy before the LORD.

—PSALM 96:11–13 (NRSV)

"You will go out in joy
and be led forth in peace;
the mountains and hills
will burst into song before you,
and all the trees of the field
will clap their hands."

—ISAIAH 55:12 (NIV)

"It is not what we have that will make us a great nation;
it is the way in which we use it."

—THEODORE ROOSEVELT

"No synonym for God is so perfect as Beauty. Whether as seen carving the lines
of the mountains with glaciers, or gathering matter into stars, or planning the
movements of water, or gardening—still all is Beauty!"

—JOHN MUIR

"Those who contemplate the beauty of the earth find reserves of strength that will
endure as long as life lasts. There is something infinitely healing in the repeated
refrains of nature—the assurance that dawn comes after night,
and spring after winter."

—RACHEL CARSON

INTRODUCTION

For as long as humans can remember, we have looked at the wondrous beauty of the world and sought to understand our place under the stars. In the tallest peaks of the mountains we see transcendence, a thin place between ourselves and the heavens. Verdant valleys remind us of the abundance the earth provides. Desert landscapes can leave us alone with our thoughts, perhaps to ponder our lives and to have gratitude for the supplies we need to sustain us in an otherwise unforgiving place. Roaring oceans remind us of the untamed power of the natural world and forces that can be mitigated but never fully controlled. Soaring birds and quick-footed deer give us over to dreams about what it would be like to move as they do, gliding on the wind's whispers or nimbly navigating rough terrain. We see beauty in these places and events; sometimes we see, or at least feel, something else our eye cannot fully see nor our mind fully understand.

These are holy moments. These moments are why we have written this book: to name not only the specific places we, the American people, have set aside as national treasures but also to speak humility and wonder and awe and gratitude into moments such as when you peer over the rim of the Grand Canyon, travel to another time in a Shenandoah hollow, or

Green sea turtle, Biscayne National Park

breathe in the smell of the earth deep in the Olympic Peninsula. How can we more fully take in what we are seeing, something that mere photographs can never record?

For many of us, those thin moments of divine connection and revelation are in the significant events of our lives: births, marriages, deaths, transitions of all kinds. They are in the everyday joys: a night at the symphony, narrowly avoiding disaster, and watching our children act with compassion, mercy, and curiosity. They are in the times when we retreat quietly somewhere to watch the dawn's early light or the dusk's lingering glow.

And for many of us, those holy moments of wonder come in America's national parks.

Seeing the fantasyland of Carlsbad Caverns through the eyes of a third-grader.

Oberholtzer Trail, Voyageurs National Park

Watching the Perseid meteor shower in Yellowstone's starlit darkness as Old Faithful erupts just a few yards away.

Lamenting wildfire smoke obscuring the afternoon view of Crater Lake and feeling ecstasy the next morning on seeing blue clear skies over the lake.

Listening to the deepest ocean depths as Atlantic waves pound the Acadia coast.

Shielding your face from the intense heat of a Hawaiian volcano's lava.

Locking eyes with a sea turtle as you snorkel in the reefs around Dry Tortugas.

Hopefully you've been, or will soon be, blessed to have those kinds of remarkable moments—moments when the pressure of packing a month's worth of sights into an afternoon, the buzz of stressed tourists and snack-craving children showing their exhaustion, the gnawing reminder that you should have eaten a while ago—when all those distractions suddenly evaporate and you see the handiwork of God right then, right there, right in front of you.

America's Holy Ground: 61 Faithful Reflections on Our National Parks seeks to reconnect you with your own holy moments of your past, to create new holy moments on future visits, or simply to transport you to any of the sixty-one national parks. Each reflection focuses on a particular theme that matches the park's natural setting or history. We have tried to give you a flavor of each park with brief notes about the features of each location, without turning it into a travelogue narrative. There are other books for that. At the same time, we have not attempted to answer all of the epistemological questions of the origin of the universe! The spiritual reflections are a starting place, not a deep theological dissertation. Every devotional closes with three questions that will help you reflect on the reading, your own faith and life story, and how you can use those reflections in the future.

Where's Mount Rushmore?

It's in South Dakota! But we know what you really mean is, "Why isn't Mount Rushmore included here?" This book covers national parks and *only* national parks. Mount Rushmore is a national monument. There are 418 national park units, including battlefields, historical sites, parkways, preserves, recreation areas, wild and scenic rivers, seashores . . . there are a lot of them, and we can't cover them all. (Yet.)

According to the National Park Service (NPS) website, "Generally, a national park contains a variety of resources and encompasses large land or water areas to help provide adequate protection of the resources." Other definitions suggest national parks offer a variety of activities like hiking, camping, fishing, and so on. It's a little vague, but why limit the possibilities?

So no, there are no national monuments in this book. But there are some parks that may be totally unfamiliar to you, including the seven Alaskan parks born on a single day in December 1980, plus the most recent addition of Indiana Dunes National Park in February 2019. All sixty-one national parks are here, including the year each was established. And when the sixty-second park is created, we'll post that on

Starfish at a Rialto Beach tide pool, Olympic National Park

our website, www.Americas-HolyGround.com.

You'll notice that forty-five of the parks have four pages devoted to them, while sixteen have two pages. We made this decision based on the number of visitors each park has. Great Smoky Mountain deserves a bit more attention than Gates of the Arctic. Forgive us if we slighted your favorite park.

A spot for reflection along the South Rim of Grand Canyon National Park

Suggestions for Using This Book

Most of us don't get to visit our national parks often enough. Our lives are too busy or the parks are too far away or the weather doesn't suit us. And that's fine. *America's Holy Ground* helps you make the most of the visits you take—and of the times when you're reminiscing or planning ahead.

Important to remember is that the land all around you has been sacred for a long, long time, longer than you can possibly imagine. This applies even in your own hometown. Native Americans have lived in North America for tens of thousands of years, and their faith practices, legends, and histories are the first human chapters in the stories of America's national parks. Respect the holy ground of those who preceded you, just as you hope others respect your holy ground. When you learn about Native American religions and traditions, contemplate how they compare and contrast with your own.

If you're visiting a national park, read the entry the night before you go or in the morning on which you're getting ready to visit. Don't wait until you get into the bustle of the park to orient yourself toward the holy. Later in the day, read the entry again. Then, if you have time and energy, read it that evening to pull everything into perspective.

If you're visiting a national park with children, read the entry aloud to those able to understand it. It may help them get ready for the cool things they're going to see, and you may be able to talk through the different themes. Change the music on the radio to something less distracting, or do the opposite: build a national parks playlist, a soundtrack for your visit. Or consider turning off the radio and all electronics when you enter a national park, especially visually stimulating devices. Incredible things are happening just outside those windows! You might even make a game of being the first to spot some anticipated landmark or resident wildlife.

If you're reading this at home, read it along with other books about national parks or find videos to see the bigger picture. This book is by no means comprehensive, nor is it meant to be, so make the most of your park experience. You may want to read the entry after you've absorbed the magnificent photography and writing in those other books. Take time to think through the questions, to center yourself and see the bigger picture.

If you're reading with a group, pick a few parks at a time. Allow fifteen to thirty minutes per park, share experiences you've had at the different parks, and share your responses to the questions. If you're really fired up, bring out the photo albums and slideshows!

Different Ways to Respond to This Book

We hope that each reflection will resonate with you in some way. We've asked open-ended questions, and the answers will be your own and nobody else's. Only you can say whether you've answered well or poorly, for the only right answer is an honest answer. Allow yourself to be vulnerable and hear the Holy Spirit moving around you.

If you're inspired, discover your own themes in national parks or neighborhood parks. Every recreational space has its own unique traits. What is it about that park with the big slide and the sandbox that makes it special? Or the one with the climbable rocks near the creek? Or the one with all the basketball goals? Discover the themes in your own neighborhood as well.

A foggy morning on the Appalachian Trail, Shenandoah National Park

If you disagree with a theme we identified, think about why that is. Many of these themes could have been used interchangeably, but perhaps you have a different experience of a park and would think differently about our interpretation.

If you are moved to act, act. That may mean sharing good news with a long-lost friend or reaching out to heal a rift. Repairing broken relationships is a worthy spiritual practice, but it must be tempered with wisdom on how best to engage the process.

If you enjoy this book or it inspires you, tell a friend. Tell your local bookstore. Write a review on Amazon or anywhere else you find reviews. Share it with our social media. See www.AmericasHolyGround.com for links. Give the book as a gift to a fellow national park lover. Share your discovery with the world.

We hope you find inspiration, motivation, and hope in these pages and everywhere you seek them. Thank you for adding this book to your journey. Now on to the parks!

The sun first rises on the United States at Cadillac Mountain.

ACADIA NATIONAL PARK

MAINE • 1919 • BEGINNINGS

Then God said, "Let there be light"; and there was light.
And God saw that the light was good; and God separated the light from
the darkness. God called the light Day, and the darkness God called Night.
And there was evening and there was morning, the first day.

—Genesis 1:3–5 (NRSV)

Listing national parks alphabetically, Acadia is at the beginning. It also begins a list of parks in the eastern part of the country. The park actually had its beginnings with a different name: *Lafayette*. It received its current moniker ten years later. Unlike western parks that have origins with presidential encounters and endorsements, Acadia owes its beginning, at least in part, to an eleven-thousand acre donation by John D. Rockefeller Jr. Folks with names like Astor, Carnegie, and Vanderbilt came to this rocky coast of Maine to get away from the hassles and heat of the city, and once others started to follow, those original families wanted to protect the natural habitat they had originally come to enjoy. Whether it was prompted by self-interest or philanthropy, their legacy is one of preservation. Many can now enjoy the wonders of this land because the powerful of their day used their influence to guard its wonders.

America's first generation of the rich and famous may have been the modern developers of Mount Desert Island (about 60 percent of which is included in the park's boundaries), but in the beginning it was the Wabanaki Indians who roamed the land carved by retreating glaciers seventeen thousand years ago. The landscape the glaciers left behind is rugged and steep and beautiful. From the coastal cliffs you peer down into narrow inlets of the North Atlantic Ocean where rough waters put on a spectacular display of spray and froth as they become

25

trapped against the land. You can venture on foot or by bike along the carriage roads that traverse fifty miles of the park, or you can hike (or drive) to the top of Cadillac Mountain. Here, from the highest vantage point along the Northeastern Seaboard, you can see the start of each day. Sunrise each day stretches along the coast of Maine, and from early October to early March, this is the first place in the continental United States to greet the sun, so the beginning of each day is truly marked here.

New beginnings are powerful, whether they mark a literal new day or the start of one thing and therefore the end of another—the start of a job, a relationship, an attitude, a habit, or a place to call home. In

Waves crash into the coast at Ship Harbor

the religious world, there are a host of seasons and events that have the feeling of a "fresh start." The beginning of Lent, a season of reflection on the broken nature of ourselves and the world; the beginning of Advent, a time of expectation

Carriage Road Bridge

that through a power beyond our own, wholeness might prevail in the created order; the beginning of a sensitivity to the Spirit in rituals such as baptism and confirmation; the beginning of a new way of being in relationship via marriage; and the transition to a new way of living in the ongoing presence of the Divine through death—an end met with a beginning.

Talk to anyone in a twelve-step program or who has been diagnosed with cancer, and they will tell you beginnings matter. Successful beginnings are so important that they become anniversaries in the future, a way of marking that something is different now than it was before. And when you have made a mistake or need forgiveness, who doesn't want or need a "do-over" kind of beginning?

It's a new day for sure, and not just on top of the pink granite knob overlooking Frenchman's Bay! Every good story, including yours, starts with a beginning.

Can you mark an important "beginning" in your life? Is there something that you would like to start over or begin afresh today? Regarding your relationships, is there space to create a "new day" with someone?

AMERICAN SAMOA
NATIONAL PARK

AMERICAN SAMOA • 1988 • ENDINGS

For now we see in a mirror, dimly, but then we will see face to face.
Now I know only in part; then I will know fully, even as I have been fully known.
—1 Corinthians 13:12 (NRSV)

If Acadia, the first park to see the sunrise, is a place to think about beginnings, then American Samoa, the last park to see the sunset, is an appropriate place to consider endings. At fourteen degrees south of the equator, this is the farthest south of any national park, and it is the only one that is leased, not owned, by the National Park Service. American Samoa is managed in cooperation with the local villages, which jointly determine park usage and construction.

If you enjoy deep blue waters, coral reefs, white sand beaches, tropical rain forests, and friendly people, this is a visit you won't want to end.

To gaze out upon an endless sea as it touches an infinite horizon is to be given the wide space for wonder. Beauty like this and a thousand wondrous acts of being human may leave us like Paul, hoping that what has already been revealed is but a shadow of what is on the other end of our faith.

Is life a prelude, or is it the finale of the great symphony of creation? Do we step out into more, grasped by infinite grace, or do we release all there is to our existence or something else? Is it *the* end, or just the end of *one* way of being?

A sea-level view of Ofu Island

Delicate Arch

ARCHES NATIONAL PARK

UTAH • 1971 • CONNECTION

A friend loves you all the time.
A brother is always there to help you.
—PROVERBS 17:17 (ICB)

Your favorite oceanside beach may look very different in a few hundred million years.

About three hundred million years ago, Arches National Park lay beneath a salty sea. Each time the sea ebbed, a layer of salt was deposited, eventually hundreds of feet thick. Then, about 160 million years ago, sand dunes lined the inland sea, covering the salt. Over time, sediment buried this sand and salt, and its crushing weight transformed it into sandstone more than a mile thick in places. That sediment also pressured the salt, warping and buckling the rock above.

Then water got to work, seeping into cracks, eroding the salt but leaving the tougher rock. Geologic shifts and hydraulic erosion chipped grooves in the rock, and the deeper-buried rock was washed away. Hard rock on top, soft rock on bottom—that won't last long, geologically speaking.

Eventually, the salt layer washed away completely, and the sandstone was left hanging over an empty gap: an arch.

In Arches National Park, this happened more than two thousand times. At least that many arches have been discovered within the boundaries of this compact park, an astonishing number. The National Park Service defines an arch as spanning at least three feet, and some of the most famous arches span hundreds of feet, a mind-boggling feat of natural engineering.

Delicate Arch is the most famous of the park's landmarks. Perched atop a ridge, the sixty-foot-tall arch is breathtaking at any time of day, though it shows off its coral colors particularly well at sunrise and

The Spectacles

sunset. A short hike gives you a view from a mile away, and a longer, tougher hike provides a perspective you'll never forget. You can see the layers within the rock: a horizontal stripe of rock or erosion on one leg of the arch, then the empty hold-your-breath space, and then the rest of the stripe on the other side. Delicate is the perfect name for it; despite being made of solid rock, the emptiness creates a sense of suspense—how long can this arch last?

Trails lead you to some of the most beloved sites in the National Park System. Landscape Arch, a ribbon of rock spanning roughly three hundred feet, makes you wonder: *Will this will be the wind that topples the arch?* Balanced Rock is exactly what its name implies—a gravity-defying feat that begs to be photographed. The 112-foot-tall span of Double Arch, with two arches sharing a base, is the park's tallest. From a certain point of view, North Window and South Window align around a nose-shaped rock, together appropriately dubbed the Spectacles. The Devil's Garden Trail leads to the Navajo Arch, with its irresistible sense of a gateway to another world. Double O Arch is the rarity of two arches in a single vertical space, a large gap with a smaller arch tucked beneath. Partition Arch, Black Arch, Tunnel Arch, and Pine Tree Arch are also along this trail.

Arches is a fragile place. These arches aren't going to last forever. Two well-known arches, Skyline and Landscape, have had significant rock collapses over the years. Wall Rock, a graceful, well-known span of more than seventy feet, wasn't so lucky; it collapsed into a pile of boulders one night in 2008. Each and every arch will eventually collapse, a reminder of our own mortality.

In some spots, even the soil on the ground is fragile. Cryptobiotic soil is a blend of bacteria, algae, lichens, moss, fungi, and other organisms. This symbiotic ecosystem reduced erosion and creates the chemistry that may allow a plant to take root. Yet one footstep can destroy it all. Hiking is restricted in many areas to protect the arches, this soil, and the hikers themselves.

As you look at the unending series of arches, inevitably your eyes will wander up one side of an arch, across the top, and down the other, thinking about the suspended rock connecting the two sides. How does that connection remain? What would it take to break that connection?

Humans are different. We have the skills to keep those connections intact—and to strengthen those connections. We have common interests, common beliefs, common needs.

What connections have made a difference in your life so far? What connections would you like to make? With whom can you connect, or reconnect, in a way that enriches you both?

Courthouse Towers

Norbeck Pass

BADLANDS NATIONAL PARK

SOUTH DAKOTA • 1978 • WISDOM

Let perseverance finish its work so that you may be mature and complete,
not lacking anything. If any of you lacks wisdom, you should ask God,
who gives generously to all without finding fault, and it will be given to you.

— JAMES 1:4–5 (NIV)

How did such a breathtakingly beautiful place get the name *Badlands*? From life-and-death lessons: it's not an easy place to live. While water is responsible for much of the erosion, water isn't always available in its present dry climate. It has also long been a difficult place to traverse, and the Lakota were the first to use the derogatory *mako sica* ("lands bad") name.

During World War II, the southern section of the park, known as the Stronghold Unit, was an Army gunnery range, and portions of the park are still unsafe for exploration due to unexploded ordnance.

When you peer out at the Badlands, you see up to seventy-five million years of history. The fossil record at Badlands is world-renowned, and paleontologists return to the park year after year to examine the fossils and search for undiscovered species. Like all national parks, it is illegal to remove anything or disturb the environment, no matter how fascinating, so seek out a park ranger or other expert if you want to understand the fossil record better.

What will likely catch your attention, though, are the layers of different colors on the eroded landscape. Bathed in earth tones of reds and browns and beiges, yellows and blacks and grays, Badlands captures that palette in countless hills with pinnacles, gullies, spires, and vistas that spread over hundreds of square miles. Each rock layer captures a different era, a different environment, a different time in the life of our world that we can experience only through the memory contained in the dirt and rock. So let's go back in time a little bit.

Geologists tell us that seventy-five million years ago what we now know as the Great Plains was the bottom of a shallow inland sea. The black Pierre Shale—the bottom layer of the rock formations—was created by sediment settling out of seawater. Fossilized sea reptiles, clams, and ammonites were preserved in this bottom layer, but they would have to wait a long time before seeing sunlight again. A lot more rock was on the way.

Eventually, the sea drained when the nearby Black Hills and the more distant Rocky Mountains rose to the west, and draining the sea exposed the black ocean mud to air. Yellow and pink mounds throughout the park are made of aerated fossil soil called paleosol.

Then, roughly thirty-five million years ago, the gray deposits of the Chadron Formation were left by flooding rivers in a subtropical forest. In this warm, lush setting roamed early mammals and the titanothere, an animal that looked like a rhino but was closer biologically to a horse. These, too, were fossilized and preserved. Layer upon layer, experience upon experience.

About thirty-two million years ago, the climate dried and cooled, and an open savannah evolved. The brown and tan sandstone of the Brule Formation marks the beds of rivers that drained from the Black Hills. The red accents in this layer are more paleosol—different materials but the same origin as the layer's yellow cousin.

Two million years later, volcanic Rockyford Ash coated the area, a distinct marker in the geologic record. The lighter-colored Sharps

Mammatus clouds over the Badlands

Sunset over the Badlands

Formation formed about twenty-nine million years ago as water and wind carried dirt and dust into the area.

In the following years, streams descending from the Black Hills meandered across the landscape, depositing soil across the flatland that still resembled the floor of the shallow inland sea. Only in the last half a million years did water and rain begin their work of carving out the park we see today. The streams flowed into the Cheyenne River, which dug a river valley that continued harnessing other streams. The concentrated water and the prairie wind combined to carve the intricate, fascinating spires and color-drenched landscapes that epitomize Badlands National Park in our current era.

Our own lives have similar eras—childhood, adolescence, young adulthood, parenthood, being empty-nesters, and so on—and each of our stories is unique in its own way, coloring our lives differently from our family's and friends' lives. Learning from our mistakes and celebrating our successes, we layer lesson upon lesson. If we learn from our experiences, we become wise. We will never know everything, of course, but we may know exactly what somebody else needs to know at a turning point in their life story. In that moment, to that person, our wisdom is priceless.

Who in your life have you considered to be wise? What qualities impress you as wise? What wisdom do you have to share with the world—or with just one other person?

BIG BEND NATIONAL PARK

TEXAS • 1944 • BORDERS

And so he brought them to the border of his holy land,
to the hill country his right hand had taken.

—PSALM 78:54 (NIV)

Big Bend National Park is tucked away in southwestern Texas, far from anything. It's so removed from cities, it was recognized in 2012 for having the darkest nighttime skies in the contiguous forty-eight states. Big Bend is hard to reach, but the Rio Grande has been working for eons to create scenery to make the long trip worthwhile.

The Rio Grande gives water to almost 1,900 miles of three states, but it is best known as the boundary between the United States and Mexico. With headwaters in Colorado, it flows within a few miles of Santa Fe, once the capital of the New Spain colony that sprawled from Wyoming to Texas to California. A decade after Texas's revolution from Mexico, when the Lone Star State joined the union, the United States deemed the Rio Grande the border, while Mexico recognized a river farther north. The 1846–1848 Mexican-American War, which cost more than thirteen thousand American lives (lost mostly to disease), settled the border at the Rio Grande.

In its ability to craft natural beauty, the Rio Grande merits recognition beyond borders.

The river flows through the Chihuahuan Desert, to some evoking stark images of barren, lifeless wasteland. Nature lovers, though, will see a diverse ecosystem with more species of birds, cacti, and bats than any other national park. The Chisos Mountains, in the heart of the park, are home to black bears and mountain lions amid a mountain-like forest of ponderosa pine, fir, cypress, oak, and aspen. Between the desert and the mountains sprawl grasslands.

The Rio Grande in Mariscal Canyon

Sunset over Mule Ears Peaks

The Rio Grande has proven itself to be quite the canyon-cutter. Big Bend National Park alone boasts three impressive canyons with depths surpassing fifteen hundred feet: Santa Elena, Mariscal, and Boquilla. For 135 million years, the river has cut through uprisings of soft limestone to create the gaps that draw floaters and canoers to the shadowy canyon floors. Sustained by the water flowing from the mountains, lush trees and vegetation line both riverbanks.

International law has established the middle of the Rio Grande channel as the border. Spend any time on a river at all and you'll know your boat will likely veer back and forth across the channel with the currents. Flowing downstream, with the United States on your left and Mexico on your right, you probably won't know how many times you leave and reenter the United States on a single float. When your float ends, be prepared for a discussion with the Border Patrol.

At the many river put-in points, seeing Mexico is simple—skipping a rock to another country is within the realm of possibility. The Boquillas Border Port of Entry, in the park's eastern section, is the only official border crossing location, but the park has its share of unofficial entry points from the south as well. Mexican craftsmen have been known to leave their wares on the northern bank in hopes that tourists will buy a souvenir. Such items are considered contraband by border officials and can be confiscated. Occasionally immigrants are spotted in the park, having successfully crossed the river, hoping to start anew in America. Immigration is an issue as old as America itself, and Big Bend is a national park where international goodwill and homeland security clash.

Parks on America's borders are places where *border* can have several definitions. Borders can be very real, like the tranquil Rio Grande flowing to the ocean. Borders can be perceived, like the prohibition against buying harmless trinkets. Or borders can be altogether imaginary, like those separating one people from another.

Where have you intentionally created borders in your life? How have you decided your own life's borders and how they are enforced? Are there borders you need to shift or erase?

One river, two countries

Mandalay Shipwreck

BISCAYNE NATIONAL PARK

FLORIDA • 1980 • CHAOS

In the beginning when God created the heavens and the earth,
the earth was a formless void and darkness covered the face of the deep,
while a wind from God swept over the face of the waters.

—GENESIS 1:1–2 (NRSV)

D o you ever imagine what it would be like to swim in the aquar-
ium in your dentist's office—you know, the one with the brightly
colored fish and the sunken ship buried in the gravel bottom? Biscayne
National Park is your chance to realize that fantasy, as 95 percent of this
park is underwater! To experience it, trade your car for a boat and your
hiking shoes for swim fins. Biscayne includes a portion of the world's
third-largest coral reef, dozens of shipwrecks, crystal clear water, and
a coastline of mangrove forest. Boating, fishing, bird-watching, scuba
diving, paddling a canoe, and catching some sun rays are all a peaceful
getaway within sight of the Miami skyline.

Large piles of discarded welk and conch shells that archeologists call
middens are evidence that humans have been drawn here since long before
the interstate made access to southern Florida "a thing." The first to
inhabit and settle in this area were Native Americans, now historically
referred to as the Glades Culture. Later, a more distinct people, the
Tequesta, leveraged the bounty of the sea to engage in trade; because it
was easier to exploit than traditional agriculture, they had more time
to develop an artisan and religious culture. They have left a record of
their presence here.

This is a park that was born out of struggle. Sites that are a wonder to
behold and worthy of preserving are also the deep desire of developers
who know the price people will pay to own a piece of land with a marvelous view. The 1950s and '60s brought a pitched battle between those

The submerged beauty of Biscayne's reef community: coral reef and moon jellyfish

who wanted to build a city with deep water industrial ports and those who wanted to conserve this pristine environment as a legacy to be enjoyed into the future. It was a bitter contest of wills that included the building of the "Spite Highway," a six-lane-wide, seven-mile-long stretch that bulldozed the middle of Elliott Key with the goal of rendering it less appealing to preserve. However, plans for future development officially came to an end, and the road has been largely reclaimed by nature. It is now the only walking path in Biscayne, meandering through a marine forest that is a great place to view wildlife.

Most people come to view Biscayne's turquoise tranquility, but for divers the scuttled ships beneath the surface belie the permanence of this placid state. When the sea is whipped up by wind and currents, it becomes a boiling cauldron of tempest and tragedy. The sunken ships are a major attraction for those who visit aquatic Biscayne. Hurricanes have scoured clean the structures built upon the Keys, and the fierce fury of the storms has claimed the lives of those who thought they could stand or sail against it.

This is perhaps the condition that the writer of the creation poem in Genesis considered when claiming that God's spirit moved over "the deep." The Hebrew concept of *tahom* (the "deep") is the origin of the chaotic forces that thrash and disturb and are unwieldy and untamable. Many scholars assert that the creating in which God engages in Genesis 1:1 is not from out of "nothing" but from the ordering of "what already is" that exists in chaos. What makes this story unique from the perspective of its ancient origin is that God does this simply by *speaking*. "Let there be Light"; "Let there be a dome;" "Let the waters be gathered into one place and let the dry land appear." It is not a violent act, nor is it fraught with labor. Such is the power of the God of the Abrahamic faiths.

In the ordering of things, the potential for each thing is realized in a peaceful and lovely way. Order allows for beauty, but chaos is the raw substance from which such splendor comes. Can you trace the lines in your life that moved from chaos to beauty? What potential beauty lies within your current experience of chaos or disruption? Over what do you have power to bring order for yourself or others?

Boca Chita Key with the Miami skyline in the distance

Dragon Point

BLACK CANYON OF THE GUNNISON NATIONAL PARK

COLORADO • 1999 • TURBULENCE

God is our refuge and strength,

an ever-present help in trouble.

Therefore we will not fear,

though the earth give way

and the mountains fall into the heart of the sea,

though its waters roar and foam

and the mountains quake with their surging.

—PSALM 46:1–3 (NIV)

Over the past fifteen million years, the Gunnison River has cut through soft volcanic ash and sedimentary rock, then through tough, ancient metamorphic rock to create one of the world's deepest and narrowest gorges. Black Canyon is so narrow that even on the days with the longest daylight, some parts of the canyon receive just half an hour of direct sunlight. At its deepest, Black Canyon of the Gunnison is 2,700 feet below the rim—half a mile down. In a state that is full of steepness, Painted Wall is Colorado's tallest cliff, a drop of 2,250 feet. In the near-eternal darkness on the canyon floor flows the Gunnison River. The tight canyon, huge boulders, and a deep downhill slope create several Class V river rapids, the most challenging and dangerous. Riding the river is a turbulent, dangerous experience.

Sometimes life's turbulence is predictable and sometimes it is not. How we react can make all the difference.

What is your initial reaction when you encounter turbulence? Are there ways to respond to turbulence that serve you better than others? How can you best help others when they encounter turbulence of their own?

BRYCE CANYON NATIONAL PARK

Suddenly a sound like the blowing of a violent wind came from heaven and filled the whole house where they were sitting. . . . All of them were filled with the Holy Spirit and began to speak in other tongues as the Spirit enabled them. . . . When they heard this sound, a crowd came together in bewilderment, because each one heard their own language being spoken. Utterly amazed, they asked: "Aren't all these who are speaking Galileans? Then how is it that each of us hears them in our native language? . . . [W]e hear them declaring the wonders of God in our own tongues!" Amazed and perplexed, they asked one another, "What does this mean?"

—ACTS 2:2–12 (NIV)

A vocabulary lesson will enrich your visit to Bryce Canyon National Park.

Usually that means learning new words. Begin this lesson, though, by learning the accurate meaning of a word you already know: *canyon*. A canyon is a valley cut by a river or stream. The Grand Canyon and the Black Canyon of the Gunnison are correctly named as canyons. Bryce Canyon is not.

Yes, Bryce Canyon is affected by water, but that water falls from the sky as rain or snow, trickling down the slope, washing away the soft, exposed limestone and other rocks. Precipitation and wind are to thank for Bryce Canyon's existence and its abundance of oddly shaped, beautifully painted rock formations that make it a gem in the National Park System.

Bryce Canyon is a collection of hoodoos, fins, spires, and other rock formations. Hold on: before you search the dictionary, here's what each of those means:

+ A hoodoo is a pillar of rock, often with a unique, bizarre shape left by erosion. You will see thousands of hoodoos at Bryce. You

Hoodoos in Bryce Amphitheater

might find yourself saying *hoodoo* thousands of times too. Feel free—it's a fun word!

+ A fin is a thin, freestanding wall of sandstone. Think of a shark's fin sticking up from its body.

+ A spire is a tall steeple-like structure, often with a pointed top.

Back to Bryce Canyon, a collection of hoodoos, fins, spires, and other rock formations drawn together in amphitheaters, bowl-shaped areas where these geological shapes cluster. Bryce has fourteen amphitheaters, of which the eponymous Bryce Amphitheater is the most popular. If you have the opportunity, get up early and revel in the dawn of a new day. The shadows frolic behind the hoodoos, altering your depth perception, changing the pinks and oranges and creams and rusts and taupes and salmons and corals almost by the second, especially if clouds imbue the sunlight with their own unique qualities. It may be the best-spent hour of your trip.

Now that you're awake and ready to go, hit the trails and have a close-up look at the hoodoos. You'll never find two alike. In the Bryce

Rainbow Point

Amphitheater, look for the Alligator, an eroded fin with a layer of white dolomite; the Wall of Windows, a collection of natural arches; and Thor's Hammer for the comic-book lovers in your group. Enjoy the hush at shadow-shrouded Silent City, and keep your eyes open for California condors that sometimes soar overhead. The Queen's Garden Trail provides an audience with Queen Victoria and her court, a prominent collection of spires. If you're not up for a hike, go on horseback. Remember that the horses know the trail better than you do; they're not going to stumble over the edge.

In the big picture of the National Park System, Bryce is a small park, just fifty-six square miles, and it's a thin ribbon of park. The Scenic Drive, with its many pullouts, provides a way to see the whole canyon.

Sunrise may have meant an early wake-up call, but don't miss sunset at Sunset Point, which may be the trailer before the truly amazing sky show. Bryce has some of the darkest skies around. Without light pollution, three times as many stars are visible in the night sky. If you're lucky enough to be at Bryce on a clear, moonless night, you will have an experience words can't describe: seeing your shadow by *starlight* millions and billions of years old. It may leave you speechless.

Bryce is a landscape so unique, it almost creates its own language. You will see colors you can't name, shapes you can't define, and natural marvels you can't describe. Fortunately, we share a language that helps us communicate our experiences of our world. Our communities have their own language: local landmarks, experiences, events, even accents bending how words sound. Even though we don't always speak the same language, God is at work when we try to describe the indescribable. After all, we're doing the same thing when we talk about God in the first place.

When have you have triumphed over a language barrier? Have you learned a language that helps you in your work, your community, or your life? What language would you like to learn so that you can communicate with somebody important to you?

CANYONLANDS NATIONAL PARK

UTAH • 1964 • STORIES

The beginning of the good news about Jesus the Messiah, the Son of God,
as it is written in Isaiah the prophet:
"I will send my messenger ahead of you,
who will prepare your way—
a voice of one calling in the wilderness,
'Prepare the way for the Lord, make straight paths for him.'"
And so...

—MARK 1:1–4 (NIV)

Phantomlike figures, nearly two dozen of them, with heads and bodies but no arms or legs, gaze silently from a mural painted on a stone cliff.

The maroon depictions in the Great Gallery are different sizes, have different adornments in a variety of stripes or patterns or shadings, and a few have faces with expressions that leave us baffled: Are they scared? Angry? Grieving? Bigger than life, the tallest exceeds seven feet in height, and the whole illustration stretches two hundred feet horizontally.

These depictions in the Great Gallery have guarded Horseshoe Canyon for a long time, and there is archeological evidence that different artists added images over hundreds or even thousands of years. The images are both pictographs painted onto the rock and petroglyphs chiseled out with a tool. It's a multimedia work, and it's not graffiti. Similar work has been uncovered at sites not too far away, and North America is dotted with native art. But at Canyonlands National Park, the Great Gallery is by far the best-known work of the long-ago artist, or artists, who left no hint of the characters, plot, or lesson of the story we marvel at today—at least no hint we can detect.

Is it a progressive story, a comic book writ large, with characters and a plotline? A primitive family portrait, marking the home of those who lived in the area for thousands of years? A religious vision of the angels and saints and spirits surrounding them? A message or warning for those who would come later?

Nobody alive knows the actual story or stories, and perhaps it's better that way. Casting our eyes upon the story that remains untold empowers our imagination, fuels our curiosity, and draws us into the mind of the artist. Not knowing the story compels us to discover our own story in the mural, and then to share it with others. Perhaps the whole point of the Great Gallery was to inspire new stories for the lucky ones who get to see it with their own eyes.

You will have lots of time to create your own story as you explore Canyonlands National Park, one of the least accessible parks in the continental United States. In the heart of the park, two great western rivers meet: the Green flows into the Colorado. Separately, the two streams are often placid. Together, they can create exhilarating rapids and, eventually, the Grand Canyon.

The Y-shaped drainage basin also creates three unique areas of the park. The most visited section is Island in the Sky, located at the park's

Ruins of Fort Bottom

northern edge, closest to the highways crossing the sparsely populated plateau. Atop the mesa is Upheaval Dome—not a dome but rather a crater from a meteorite that smashed

On the Colorado River

into the earth around sixty million years ago.

From Island in the Sky, you can see the rivers' confluence and peer across to the other two areas. The Needles, in the park's southeastern area, was named for its slender sandstone columns. Elephant Hill is a well-known challenge for off-road drivers and bicyclists. To the west is The Maze, undeveloped and a long drive from anywhere. If you've ever wondered what it would be like to live on another planet without water or food or fuel, consider visiting the Maze—and plan well.

The Great Gallery is in the Horseshoe Canyon Unit, northwest of the park and a good haul from the park's visitor centers and civilization. The challenging trail drops more than seven hundred feet to the mute figures on the cliff wall, but your imagination will thank you for the effort. Just think of the story you'll have to tell when you get home!

Our faith is built around stories. From the creation story through the nation of Israel, the gospels and the beginning of the church, all the way through to fantasy-like Revelation, the Bible is a revered collection of faith stories that provide inspiration and guidance our whole life long. Its stories shape who we become—and we all have a story to tell.

What are the stories you remember from when you were young, whether you liked them or despised them? What stories give you enjoyment or inspiration or solace? What do you want the story of your life to be?

CAPITOL REEF NATIONAL PARK

UTAH • 1971 • RECONCILIATION

*Then Peter came to Jesus and asked, "Lord, how many times shall I forgive my
brother or sister who sins against me? Up to seven times?" Jesus answered,
"I tell you, not seven times, but seventy-seven times."*

—MATTHEW 18:21–22 (NIV)

Earth broke open at Capitol Reef National Park. Enclosing a
hundred-mile-long fracture in the earth's crust, Capitol Reef is
a stark reminder of how dramatically things can change. Eons at sea level
resulted in ten thousand feet of sedimentary strata, layer upon layer of
different colored rock stacked atop the Colorado plateau. Then, about
seventy million years ago, most of that plateau lifted uniformly. But
in this area, that shifting reactivated a dormant fault line. The earth
split, not with a dramatic pop like you'd see in a science fiction movie,
but significantly nonetheless. Over time, the western side rose, and
today the ledge is more than a thousand feet tall. What we see now is a
giant, colorful, sprawling wall showing hundreds of millions of years
of history, including countless fossils dating back to those sea-level
years. The colors are so vivid, Native Americans named the area "land
of the sleeping rainbow."

When you get off the main highway that traverses Capitol Reef, you
drive through a sandstone valley called Waterpocket Fold. The fold
follows the seam where the valley was ripped apart. You are driving
atop earth-shaping history! You're also driving along a *monocline*, the
geological term for the stairstep created by the shift. Waterpocket Fold
is lined with sandstone that has eroded into depressions that can, for
a while, capture rain or runoff or stream water. In the middle of the
desert, anything that captures water even for a little while merits our
attention. In Capitol Reef, it merited the naming of an entire valley.

The Castle

Fruita orchard in bloom

Capitol Reef drew its name from two inspirations. *Capitol* was inspired by the white domes of Navajo sandstone, a rock that tends to erode into softer, smoother shapes that resemble the domes atop capitol buildings across the country. As for *reef,* it is not meant to evoke the coral structures in our oceans, but rather a barrier or impediment to travel. Reaching such a steep incline usually meant going around it, not an easy assignment for a hundred-mile-long ridge.

When the Mormons moved to the American West, they hoped to leave behind discrimination and violence against their new religion. Some settlers sought to create an entirely different country specifically for Mormons called Deseret. Though nestled in a beautiful setting, the Utah desert didn't necessarily suit the newcomers well. For decades, a handful of pioneer families scraped out a living by farming along the Fremont River around Fruita. Though they abandoned the village in 1955 when the National Park Service purchased the town, their work lives on in green oasis-like patches, orchards of 2,700 trees that still produce cherries, apples, peaches, pears, almonds, walnuts, and apricots, fruit you can harvest for a snack for your drive to the next stop. A settler's home, schoolhouse, barn, and farm implements remain in the area, as do descendants of those Mormon settlers.

Religious imagery influences the names of park landmarks, including Cathedral Valley, the Walls of Jericho, and the adjacent Temple of the Moon and Temple of the Sun. Driving the looped roads inside this long and skinny park gives you many opportunities to stop and explore the side canyons, petroglyphs, and rock domes.

Eventually, the Mormon settlements that could have been Deseret were welcomed into the United States as the state of Utah, a rift mended. And if given enough time, the great wall of Capitol Reef will erode and perhaps fill in the Waterpocket Fold valley. It may take a long, long time, but it is possible.

Whether that is a rift in society like racism, gender discrimination, religious persecution, or political differences, or a relational rift like an estrangement or divorce, or a personal injury that you haven't been able to get over yet, given patience, work, and time, even the widest rifts can be mended, the deepest wounds can heal. Faith can be an important tool in our recovery. Reconciliation is within our reach when we can imagine a better life, a better way of living together.

Where have you reconciled in your life? What reconciliation would help you most, and how do you think that might happen? How can you create reconciliation in your community or your family?

Waterpocket Fold from Chimney Rock Trail

Sunlight streams through the cave's natural entrance

CARLSBAD CAVERNS
NATIONAL PARK

NEW MEXICO • 1930 • IMAGINATION

God can do anything, you know—far more than you could ever imagine or guess
or request in your wildest dreams! He does it not by pushing us around but by
working within us, his Spirit deeply and gently within us.

—EPHESIANS 3:20–21 (MESSAGE)

The mesquite and sagebrush of southern New Mexico have their own beauty, especially where the Guadalupe Mountains, an ancient coral reef, have been lofted skyward by tectonic pressures.

Below ground, though, something truly unforgettable happens seven hundred feet down.

Carlsbad Caverns may be the second-best known cave in the world, after Jesus' empty tomb. This labyrinth of enormous underground rooms and passageways, speleothem sculpture created by innumerable drips of calcite-rich water, and the well-known avian residents that tipped off a young farmhand that a cave was nearby, have combined to make this hole-in-the ground a mind-boggling natural attraction for more than half a million visitors each year.

The cave chambers formed about six million years ago when a limestone reef, formed by coral in a long-vanished sea, began dissolving as slightly acidic water seeped down and reacted with hydrogen sulfide gas, created by deep petroleum deposits interacting with underground water. This combination dissolved the limestone, leaving huge holes.

Over the last five hundred thousand years, when more rain fell on the surface, water carrying dissolved calcite (the main ingredient of limestone) and other minerals seeped through the roof of the cave. Sometimes the minerals attached to cave formations hanging from the ceiling: stalactites jutting down like teeth, sheet-like draperies, or

Hall of Giants

tubular straws. Sometimes the minerals dripped and were deposited on spear-like stalagmites, more rounded flowstone. In places where the formations grew together, columns connect the ceiling and floor.

This combination went undocumented until 1898, when sixteen-year-old farmhand Jim White noticed a huge colony of bats in the evening sky. "I followed on until I found myself in a wilderness of mighty stalagmites," White later wrote in his autobiography, *Jim White's Own Story*. "It was the first cave I was ever in, and the first stalagmites I had ever seen, but instinctively I knew, for some intuitive reason, that there was no other scene in the world which could be justly compared with my surroundings." White told his neighbors, who refused to believe what he'd seen. They couldn't imagine the fantastic sights he described. Only after he led a tour for the National Geographic Society twenty-six years later did the cave gain its rightfully deserved fame. In early days, those who couldn't walk down into the cave were lowered in a waist-deep bucket dangling from a rope through a mine shaft. Today, an elevator descends 750 feet to the center of the cave, but you can still follow young Jim White's footsteps through the natural entrance.

In the subterranean wonderland, set your imagination free. The main tour leads to Big Room, an eight-acre cavern where the dome arches over sixty feet high, housing many of the best-known formations. The sixty-foot-tall Giant and the Twin Domes loom like layered pancakes dripping batter, thousands of ridges marking untold years of deposits. Rock of Ages sprawls like an alien oozing from wall crevices. Bottomless Pit isn't bottomless, but 140 feet is still pretty deep!

Thousands of stalactites and straws stained with rust adorn Painted Grotto. By itself, the Big Room feeds creativity: What would you have named these speleothems?

There's more to Carlsbad Caverns than the Big Room. The King's Palace, The Queen's Chamber, Papoose Room, and Green Lake Room, the Left Hand Tunnel, Lower Cave, and Hall of the White Giant are all available for ranger-led tours, But remember, some are harder to access than others and may challenge those uncomfortable in tight spaces. If you're up for hard-core spelunking, talk to a ranger about touring other caves in the park; so far, 120 caves have been discovered!

At the end of the day, during warmer months, stick around to see what led Jim White to the cave in the first place: hundreds of thousands of bats embarking on a night of the yummiest bugs the desert offers! If not for the bats, you'd be swatting mosquitoes, shooing away flies, and unwittingly driving past one of the most amazing sites on Earth. Or, rather, *in* Earth.

The oddities of Carlsbad Caverns stick with you. Who knew dripping water could create something so bizarre and beautiful and . . . well, weird! Standing before these natural marvels, it seems so impossible—yet there it is. God helps us to the impossible. We just have to imagine it first.

What have you imagined in the past that inspires you now? How do you imagine you can make your life or an important relationship better or healthier? How can you help others imagine limitless possibilities?

Bats begin their nightly hunt for dinner.

CHANNEL ISLANDS NATIONAL PARK

CALIFORNIA • 1980 • PROTECTION

But let all who take refuge in you be glad; let them ever sing for joy.
Spread your protection over them, that those who love your name may rejoice in you.

—PSALM 5:11 (NIV)

A chain of islands a dozen miles off the California coast, Channel Islands National Park is home to one of the country's most diverse ecosystems, on the ground, in the air, and below the water. This park sits where two currents—one warm, flowing from the equator, the other cold, flowing from the northern Pacific—meet head-on, creating a climate like no other in North America.

This climate, combined with the isolation from the coast, means that Channel Islands has fewer species than a typical habitat. But many of the animals there might not have survived if not for this park, created in part to protect the ecosystem. Channel Islands is a bird-watcher's paradise. But it's home to more than birds: almost 150 animals and plants specific to the Channel Islands, including the island fox, the spotted skunk, and two unique mice species, live nowhere else on earth. More than two thousand species coexist on these isolated islands, and that's just those who live above the water. The surrounding ocean hosts a forest of seaweed and about one-third of the world's ocean-dwelling species.

Isolation from the mainland protected these animals, but it took a disastrous 1969 oil spill, which helped spur the environmental movement, to prompt lawmakers to protect the Channel Islands officially as a national park.

When or where have you felt God's protective presence? How do you provide shelter for others in your life? How can you extend that generosity further?

Arch Point,
Santa Barbara Island

Wetlands host the largest tract of bottomland hardwood forest in the country.

CONGAREE NATIONAL PARK

SOUTH CAROLINA • 2003 • UNITY

How very good and pleasant it is
when kindred live together in unity!
—Psalm 133:1 (NRSV)

Do you have a childhood memory of catching fireflies in the early summer evening twilight? These beetles are one of a few species given the trait of bioluminescence. You can see "lightning bugs" in a great many places, but there are only a few where you can see them flash synchronously. One is in South Carolina, where the Congaree and Wateree rivers merge each year after heavy spring rains.

The floodplain hardwood forest, often misclassified as a swamp, comes alive in late May and early June with unified pluses of light and darkness after sunset. The purpose of this mysterious rhythm is unknown, but their "in sync" light show is a marvelous display. Diversity and difference have their place, but we should not underestimate the power established when things work together in unity.

Congaree offers magnificent exhibitions of natural wonder in the daylight, too, including a forest canopy of Bald Cypress, Water Tupelo, and Loblolly Pine filled with every bird native to South Carolina. The rivers, lakes, sloughs, and creeks are home to a plethora of amphibians, snakes, insects, mammals, and fish. Hike a trail or take to the water via kayak in the reverent quiet and be amazed at how all of this comes together as one.

Is unity the absence of difference? How can unity lead to beauty and strength? Is unity a prerequisite for peace?

CRATER LAKE NATIONAL PARK

OREGON • 1902 • REFLECTION

As water reflects the face,
so one's life reflects the heart.
—Proverbs 27:19 (NIV)

When you see Crater Lake, it steals your breath. How can something be so *blue*?

As you approach Crater Lake from the Oregon countryside, you see a mesa ringed with low hills. You drive up the side of the hill, through the pines. If you arrive from the north, you'll pass through a stretch of volcanic pumice where little grows. Arrivals from the south parallel the Annie Creek gorge. Even when you arrive at the top, you may not see the lake just yet. Depending on where you are, you may need to get out of your car to see it.

But when you *do* see it—oh my!

The Klamath people who lived in the area thousands of years ago believed Llao, their god of the underworld, lived in Giiwas, a twelve-thousand-foot-tall mountain whose volcanic clues may have inspired the Klamath's mythology. Almost eight thousand years ago, Giiwas (later named Mount Mazama by a mountain-climbing club) exploded in volcanic fury, leading to the collapse of the mountain. Scientists believe that what remained of the mountain's peak collapsed into its emptied magma chamber over the course of just a few weeks. Imagine what the Klamath tribes living in the area felt as a revered landmark and holy place vanished right before their eyes!

What remained of the mountain was not a crater but a caldera, a giant bowl that captures rainfall and snow. In a typical year, six-and-a half feet of precipitation rains down on the 250-square-mile lake. That should eventually cause the bowl to overflow, right? No: Crater Lake

View from Cleetwood Cove Trail

has an amazing environmental balance. The volume of the water that falls into the crater is almost identical to the amount that evaporates or leaks out through one small area of the lake bed. The surface level of Crater Lake has remained almost stable over the years that scientists have tracked that information.

That still leaves a lot of water. Surveys indicate that the deepest point is 1,943 feet deep—the deepest lake in the United States, more than three stacked Gateway Arches! Virtually no water flows in from another source, so without soil or sediment to cloud the water, it is nearly clear and pure and cold, averaging around 58 degrees Fahrenheit. When you look out at the lake of nearly pure water, you see physics at work, the water reflecting the blue light refracted out of pure white sunlight.

Only one trail, the strenuous Cleetwood Cove Trail on the northern rim, leads to the water. Descending seven hundred feet, and knowing you have to ascend those same seven hundred feet, may seem daunting, but it might be the best hike you'll ever take. Crater Lake's only boat ramp is at the foot of the trail, and only three boats ply the lake's waters seasonally; to protect the clean waters and the lake's ecology no others are allowed on the lake. A guided tour gives you the rare opportunity to peer into the seemingly bottomless waters, to see up-close Wizard Island—Giiwas's attempt at reviving its volcanic glory manifested in a conical island—and to circle Phantom Ship, a rock pillar that plays a camouflaged hide-and-seek against the rocky shore.

Crater Lake's astonishing clear water

But what may stick with you most is how the deep water mirrors all that is above it: the volcanic caldera rim, the peaks rising above the caldera, even the clouds passing overhead. Gazing at the reflection can be calming and inspiring, and it can be disconcerting and disorienting. You may be surprised at what you see.

The deepest swimming hole you'll ever find

God created humans as self-aware: we know our feelings, our histories, our successes, and our failures. We know our whole story, whether we choose to remember that story honestly or to sugarcoat the painful parts to make it easier to swallow. When used best, self-awareness and reflection help us see our actions and our choices in new ways, hopefully teaching us how to make better choices in the future. Truly reflecting on our lives requires courage to admit when we were wrong, vulnerability to admit when our actions hurt others or ourselves, and forgiveness when we acknowledge that we have sinned.

Reflect on the big choices in your life, or a surprising choice that had unexpected benefits or consequences. If you could choose again, what would you choose differently? Are there practices you engage for more meaningful reflection? How can your reflection propel you to act now or to make amends with someone you have hurt?

Sunrise

Brandywine Falls
after a heavy rain

CUYAHOGA VALLEY NATIONAL PARK

OHIO • 2000 • RESTORATION

Then the angel showed me the river of the water of life, as clear as crystal,
flowing from the throne of God and of the Lamb down the middle of the great
street of the city. On each side of the river stood the tree of life,
bearing twelve crops of fruit, yielding its fruit every month.
And the leaves of the tree are for the healing of the nations.
—REVELATION 22:1–2 (NIV)

In 1969, sparks from a train passing on a trestle spanning the river ignited oil-soaked debris floating in the Cuyahoga River. It was not the deadliest fire, nor was it the costliest, but of the more than a dozen times the river burned in the last 150 years, it was the most notable. Cleveland, the city through which the Cuyahoga winds as it reaches Lake Erie, became the butt of many a late-night comic's jokes. The once-proud industrial city, with its hardworking immigrant-filled neighborhoods representing much of central and eastern Europe, became known as the "mistake on the lake." How bad is your city if your river burns? Apparently, pretty bad.

Sometimes, in the flowing current of events and circumstance, even awful things can become a channel for something good to follow. The sight of the Cuyahoga—meaning crooked—River burning against the city skyline galvanized a growing movement of people who realized our environment was in trouble, and not just in Ohio. The inferno that lasted a little more than an hour inspired legislation that led to the establishment of the National Environmental Policy Act, the Clean Water Act, and the eventual creation of the Environmental Protection Agency. An image of a dying, burning river, choked with sewage effluent and industrial waste, validated the urgent need for the first Earth

Bald eagle with the catch of the day

Cuyahoga Valley Scenic Railroad

Day, celebrated only a year later in 1970.

Maybe it was just embarrassment, or perhaps the realization that the river should be a source of life rather than a perpetual portrait of failure was what united the communities bordering the eighty-five twisting miles of the Cuyahoga. They invested their tax dollars and a considerable amount of time and energy to clean up the crooked river that meanders from near the Pennsylvania border east of Cleveland south toward Akron and back north again and on to Lake Erie. Now, five decades after that infamous fire, the river is reborn, home to sixty species of fish. Bald eagles and blue herons soar over the tree-lined embankments where river otters and beavers make their homes.

The park is different than most of those in the National Park System. Yes, it has sweeping vistas (The Ledges), deep canyons (Tinkers Creek Gorge), waterfalls (Brandywine, Blue Hen, and Bridal Veil), and rocks aplenty (Deep Lock Quarry) that hold the geological record narrating the story of how the earth was born. But it also has working farms, ski slopes, operational canal locks, a scenic railroad, art galleries, a summer home for the Cleveland orchestra, and immediate access to the amenities of two cites and a metropolitan area of 3.5 million people—the evidence of whose close proximity is almost completely hidden from view in most areas of the park. But it is also similar to many national parks in the cooperation of many bordering communities and a desire to preserve the natural beauty. Cuyahoga Valley, unlike any other, exists not because the government thought it ought to but because the people of northeast Ohio lobbied and pestered the NPS to designate it as a park until it did so in the year 2000.

The Cuyahoga River was dead and now it lives. The river restoration is a miracle—not so much the Divine kind, but rather one brought about by the imagination (and possibly the penitence) of the people who live along its boundar-

ies. Unless, of course, you believe that God's miracles can be done by people who simply want and realize the need for change. Either way, the rebirth is something to behold and makes us wonder what else is waiting to be altered by a group of people who know that the way things are is not necessarily the way they have to be or should be.

Demonstration lock

What areas of your life have you restored? What areas are you working on right now? How can you help others restore their spirits and their lives?

Everett Road Covered Bridge

DEATH VALLEY NATIONAL PARK

CALIFORNIA AND NEVADA • 1994 • LIFE

For I am convinced that neither death, nor life, nor angels, nor rulers,
nor things present, nor things to come, nor powers, nor height, nor depth,
nor anything else in all creation, will be able to separate us from the love of
God in Christ Jesus our Lord.

—ROMANS 8:38–39 (NRSV)

Just the name, *Death Valley*, conjures up images seen through the squinted eyes of a parched prospector, clutching his empty canteen, peering up from the desert floor at an unrelenting sun and circling buzzards. *Death* Valley: too hot, too dry, too far from anywhere, and too deep for anything to survive. Scorching sand, empty riverbanks, blowing tumbleweed, and the absence of anything green is what we assume we will find here. It is after all *Death* Valley!

Nothing could be further from the truth—once you get past it being the driest (less than two inches of average rainfall per year), hottest (134 degrees, highest temperature ever recorded *on earth*), lowest (282 feet *below* sea level), and also the biggest park in the lower 48 states (5,262 square miles, more than two Delawares).

Death Valley is actually full of life. If you know where to look, you can even find water! Yes, there are scorpions and rattlesnakes, but there are also fish, birds, reptiles, mammals large and small, and vegetation that at the right time of year blooms into fields of wildflowers. That's not what you'd expect from a place with *death* in its name. It is hot and dry, but life, including human life, has adapted to these harsh conditions.

Death Valley is a place riddled with contrasts. The average daytime July temperature is 120 degrees, but for part of the year, there is snow visible in higher elevations. The desert floor is below sea level, but the tallest mountain in the park, Telescope Peak, towers 11,331 feet

Desert Gold wildflowers at sunset

A pupfish swims in the shallows of Salt Creek.

above it. Much of the park is arid, but there are numerous oases where life flourishes. It doesn't rain often, but when it does, the desert bursts with color and empty riverbanks flow with that one thing necessary for life: water.

You might expect shades of brown to dominate the color scheme, but here is another surprise: the valley is filled with colors. At one time the valley was a lake. As the waters dried, they left behind layers of sedimentation that record the memory of the water's presence in the rock. Those colors display like a rainbow of subtle hues and gentle pastels in the canyons and hillsides. Water shaped the valley as it carved its way down the mountains.

Death Valley is less than hospitable, but human communities have been here for thousands of years and found valuable resources. The Timbisha Shoshone were the first to use the valley, following seasonal migrations and gathering nuts from the pinyon pines and beans from mesquite trees. Prospectors from the 1849 gold rush sought their fortunes here, and later miners extracted borax, used in soap, cleaning products, and even pest control. Skeletons of the mines remain, as does the name "20 Mule Team Canyon Road," an homage to the way processed borate ore was hauled out of the valley to the railroad for shipment west. And there are the people, more than a million each year since the park opened, who come to be surprised how much life there is in Death Valley—as long as you know where the water is (and drink the recommended one-half to one gallon or more per day while you visit)!

With a little reflection, we can see in the living of our lives the metaphor of Death Valley. We are aware, to varying degrees, that our lives are finite. The prospect of death is a part of life. Our path is not always easy, and it is littered with disappointments of unmet expectations, broken relationships, and unrealized dreams. Sometimes the systems in which we participate damage us and other people. Aspirations lie unfulfilled and hopes diminished. Dry, low, barren, and hard-baked places are the spaces in which we sometimes find ourselves.

But amidst difficulty are signs of life-giving activity. Relationships can be mended, or new ones created. New dreams emerge. Our emotional scars are testimonies to our survival. Systems that abuse can also be called to account and, by that very action, begin to be changed. People who affirm our value are an oasis, and our faith reminds us to look around and see that—despite the current circumstances—there is more here than meets the eye. Because even in Death Valley, death does not have the last word.

When have you been too quick to judge the value of a person or place? Can you be the person who serves as an oasis to another? What (or who) brings you hope in times of despair?

Sand Dunes at Mesquite Flat

Snow-covered Alaska Range

DENALI NATIONAL PARK

ALASKA • 1917 • NAME

A good name is to be chosen rather than great riches,
and favor is better than silver or gold.

—PROVERBS 22:1 (NRSV)

The Athabaskan people who originally inhabited this land had a name for the mountain that stands as the central feature of the park: *Denali*. It translates as *Tall One*, *High One*, *Big One*, or *Geat One*. The name is fitting, given that at 20,310 feet, it is the highest mountain in North America. People who come to this massive six-million-acre preserve enjoy some of the best wildlife viewing in the world. Toklat grizzly bear, caribou, hoary marmot, wolf, moose, Dall sheep, red fox, snowshoe hare, and wolverine are frequently spotted. Wildlife is so abundant here that you can often view it from the safety and comfort of a tour bus.

If you prefer birds to mammals, there are 160 species of birds to see, from golden eagles and arctic warblers to ravens and the ubiquitous North American robin. Avian migrants to Denali for the Alaskan summer originate from exotic locations like Central and South American rain forests, the coast of Chile, and eastern Eurasia. Blackpoll warblers fly seventy-two hours nonstop from South America to breed in these boreal forests.

The park yields views of these animal wonders with ease against a backdrop of colorful fields in the spring and summer, and in winter, a scene of deep snowy white. The mountain is a different story. Winds coming off the Gulf of Alaska are laden with moisture that condenses as it moves over the mountains, forming clouds and rain. Because of this, of the half-million people who visit the park each year in hopes of gazing at Denali's formidable peak, about 70 percent leave disappointed. *High One* often hides in the mist and is revealed to only a fortunate few.

The High One

High One has left an impression on everyone who has been in its presence, especially those who were in the land before the first European prospector, Frank Densmore, for whom the mountain was briefly named, or all those who have since known it as Mount McKinley (named for President William McKinley). This is both a remarkable aspect and a similarity of so many of our national parks: lands we have set aside by Executive Order or Act of Congress were *already* revered by people who lived in these places long before we happened upon them. Too often American settlers gave themselves credit for the idea of preserving these lands, as if they were the first to see their value. And, frankly, we have inherited that misplaced pride. Native people long ago set these wonders aside as places to be treasured and preserved. Thankfully, for most Americans, preservation of their beauty rather than exploitation of their resources is still the goal. Vigilance is necessary to assure that it stays that way, as is the humility to realize that we borrow these lands from our children and all who come after us.

The reclaiming of the name *Denali* for the mountain had its share of controversy. In 1975, the Alaskan Board of Geographic Names requested that the native nomenclature be restored, but members of the Ohio delegation in Congress sought to protect the McKinley name as a tribute to the twenty-fifth president and their native son. It was not until forty years later in 2015 that the U.S. Secretary of the Interior announced that the mountain would once again be recognized by the name given it by the first people who lived in its embrace. Such an act serves as tribute to those who were here first, and it reminds us that the land was not always "ours." Some might consider this renaming as *Denali* to be a subtle act of repentance. That is appropriate.

Grizzly bear

There is power in a name. Once you know someone's name, you can get their attention if they are within earshot. The Bible supports the idea that names are both evocative and descriptive. God told Moses the Name for God in the encounter in the burning bush, and it has forever changed the relationship between the Holy One and us. Respect, recognition, identity, inclusion, and intimacy can all be communicated by a name and how it is spoken.

Aurora Borealis

Native American names dot the landscape in our country, and very likely where you live. Who are the people who lived on and named the land before you? What does it mean to give your name to someone or some cause? How do you want your name to be remembered?

DRY TORTUGAS NATIONAL PARK

The Spirit of GOD, the Master, is on me because GOD anointed me.
He sent me to preach good news to the poor, heal the heartbroken,
Announce freedom to all captives, pardon all prisoners.
—ISAIAH 61:1 (MESSAGE)

D r. Samuel Mudd spent four years behind the walls of Fort Jefferson, an island fort converted to a prison after the Civil War. In the days following the assassination of President Lincoln, he set a stranger's broken leg. Unfortunately for Dr. Mudd, that stranger was assassin John Wilkes Booth. Jurors labeled Mudd an accomplice to the assassin and sentenced him to life imprisonment on this island sixty-eight miles west of Key West.

The doctor maintained his innocence and could have made himself miserable with anger and guilt. But two years later, when yellow fever erupted on the island and the prison doctor died, Mudd stepped in and is credited with saving and inspiring his fellow inmates. He was released after serving four years, and the prison closed a decade later.

The hexagonal Fort Jefferson, a mighty brick fortress that was never completed, is now the centerpiece of Dry Tortugas National Park, named for the several species of sea turtles there and the lack of fresh water. The fort is also one of the few dry points; more than 99 percent of the park is covered in water. Sharks, fish, seabirds, coral, and turtles live in the park. Also passing through the park: Cuban refugees seeking a new start in America.

What in your life holds you captive? From what do you need to be freed? How can you help others emancipate themselves from their own prisons?

North Beach of Fort Jefferson

A great egret hunts
among the cypress.

EVERGLADES NATIONAL PARK

FLORIDA • 1947 • PRESERVATION

God blessed them and said to them, "Be fruitful and increase in number;
fill the earth and subdue it. Rule over the fish in the sea and the birds in the sky
and over every living creature that moves on the ground."
—Genesis 1:28 (NIV)

If you are asked to describe the Everglades, the words *mountains* and *valleys* are not likely to come to mind. *Swamp, wetlands*, or *grassy sea* are the images most commonly associated with the southern tip of Florida.

Park your assumptions at the gate, because the Everglades is actually quite diverse, and yes, rangers refer to "mountains and valleys" when describing the various habitats within the 1.5 million acres of the park's boundaries. There are seven distinct ecosystems, all of which exist because of subtle changes of elevation in the limestone rock on which the Everglades rest. Granted, the differences between a "mountain" and "valley" may only be a few inches, but in terms of what vegetation grows and the life it can support, these variances are remarkably significant.

The highest ground is home to the Tropical Hardwood Hammock. The name *hammock* describes dense, closed-canopied stands of broadleaf trees. The earliest preservation efforts to guard and protect these unique habitats, home for the Florida panther, the barred owl, whitetail deer, and gray fox, started in 1916 with the creation of Royal Palm State Park.

Most threatened of the habitats is the Pine Rocklands. Only 2 percent of this ecosystem is estimated to have survived the conquest of development as its elevation made it most suitable for agricultural and real estate development. Contrast this to the most prevalent habitat, the Grassland Prairie, our archetypal image of the Everglades. Dry part of the year, it becomes a slow-flowing sheet of fresh water in a "river of grass" during the wet season. It is home to alligators, fish, turtles, and wading birds when the rains come.

The Cypress Dome habitat flourishes in the limestone depressions where water can be present year-round. The primary marker of this space is the bald cypress tree, which serves as a host for bromeliads and other "air plants" and nesting birds like egrets, wild turkeys, and herons. Taller trees grow where there is plenty of moisture and peat, with smaller trees taking root around the edges of the habitat, where these qualities are less pervasive. The contrasting sizes of the trees create a dome-like appearance.

Two additional habitats include the slough (rhymes with *you*) and the mangroves. Rangers often refer to the sloughs and their seasonal cycle of "wet and dry" as the heartbeat of the park. They are the "valleys" in the shallow shelf of limestone and are water-filled year-round.

The mangroves represent the transition between fresh water that flows south from Lake Okeechobee, and salty Florida Bay and the Gulf of Mexico. Mangroves flourish in brackish conditions influenced by the presence of salt and the constant flow of the tides. In the mangroves and

Red mangrove habitat

Florida Bay, you may find the rare American crocodile living side by side with the American alligator. The bay's seagrasses and rich aquatic life thrive because of the abundant penetration of sunlight in the shallow waters that serve as the nursery for much of the Gulf of Mexico's fish and invertebrates.

The Everglades was initially set aside and preserved not because of its ostensive beauty but because its habitat, with its fragile ecosystem development, was being threatened by agricultural practice and flood-control projects by the early middle of the twentieth century. Thanks to a growing movement of environmental awareness, gradual protections stopped the infringement of unchecked development into this delicate web of water-filled wonder.

Endangered Florida panther on the prowl

The very act of preservation catches our imagination here, as if the desire to do so reflects a

Alligator swimming in search of prey

characteristic of the Divine Nature from which we spring. In the poem that opens Genesis 1, to be given dominion over creation is understood as meaning to rule in the earth the way God rules in the cosmos, meaning for the benefit and welfare of all living things. To preserve, protect, delight, and to wonder about the mysterious interconnectedness of all life may well be the echo of the Holy voice that once whispered into our ear.

In what ways have you participated in the preservation of creation? Did such an action feel sacred? Does it change your behavior when you realize the world is an interconnected web of meaning in which you cannot affect part without impacting the whole?

GATES OF THE ARCTIC NATIONAL PARK

ALASKA • 1980 • WILDERNESS

Jesus, full of the Holy Spirit,
returned from the Jordan and was led by the Spirit in the wilderness.
—LUKE 4:1 (NRSV)

You can fly in, hike in, or "mush in," but you cannot drive in! Gates of the Arctic National Park is inside the Arctic Circle, making it the most northern as well as the most remote park. It is unaltered, untamed wilderness with no roads, established trails, designated campgrounds, or cell service. Here you see the world as seven thousand years of human ancestry before you have encountered it. Caribou, grizzly and black bear, Dall sheep, musk ox, wolves, fox, and moose wander the land making the most of a short summer season, tending to the matters of making life and then moving on to escape the harshness of the long polar winter.

Abraham, Moses, Elijah, John the Baptist, Jesus, and a host of known and unknown mystics and ascetics spent time in the wilderness. Some ran *away* from the distractions of life or to break the daily routine in favor of a new way of being. Others ran *toward* an encounter with the Divine or to discover the sacred in spaces where it dwells less camouflaged by the secular. It can be a time set aside for cleansing the soul, tuning the heart, or where you listen for the Spirit whispering your name. A time and place for wonder.

What do you hope to discover in the wilderness? Is God more or less present or manifest here than elsewhere? How might the wilderness change you?

Aerial view of Brooks Range

The Gateway Arch towers 630 feet over a reflecting pond.

GATEWAY ARCH
NATIONAL PARK

MISSOURI • 2018 • ART

"You have many workers: stonecutters, masons and carpenters, as well as those skilled in every kind of work in gold and silver, bronze and iron—craftsmen beyond number. Now begin the work, and the LORD be with you."
—1 CHRONICLES 22:15–16 (NIV)

You can see the heart of America's smallest national park for miles. You catch glimpses of it from highways, on city streets, peeking out when you least expect it. Silvery, sleek, and graceful, the Gateway Arch is one of the most famous buildings in the world, yet it's still a surprise every time you see it.

Towering 630 feet over the Mississippi River in downtown St. Louis, Missouri, the Gateway Arch is an engineering marvel. A stainless-steel monument to western settlement, the Arch itself took only thirty-one months to build, climbing into the skies as two equally tall curving towers, then unified by a supporting trestle arch until the final keystone piece completed the structure in October 1966. Once the exterior was completed, a one-of-a-kind elevator with rotating cars was installed in each tower to lift visitors to an observation deck in four minutes, returning them to earth in three minutes.

The idea for this grand monument was born out of blight. During the Great Depression, the St. Louis riverfront had become rundown. Looking for ways to energize the city's core and to stimulate the local economy, civic leaders floated the idea of a national monument commemorating both Thomas Jefferson, who authorized the Louisiana Purchase that doubled the country's size, and St. Louis's ensuing role in America's growth. For decades, St. Louis had been the largest city in western America, a jumping-off point to all destinations west.

Legislation at the federal, state, and local level authorized the project, and work to clear the site began in 1936 although no monument had been decided upon. A few years later, the ninety-acre site, the original location of the French frontier town of St. Louis, had been opened up.

World War II temporarily redirected the city's energy, but the dream to build a monument held fast. In 1947, an international contest invited designs from the world's greatest architects. In Detroit, thirty-seven-year-old Eero Saarinen worked at his father's architectural firm. Born in Finland and raised in Michigan, Saarinen first gained recognition for his unique chair designs. When the St. Louis monument contest was announced, his father's firm submitted a design—and so did Eero.

Saarinen's original design used as its basic shape a catenary arch, the line created by a chain, cord, or cable when suspended from two points. His team experimented with different designs for the chain's links, but triangles, diminishing in size as the height increased, won the day. The original design proposed a slightly smaller and squashed arch, not quite as tall as it was wide.

Almost complete, September 1965

"The major concern . . . was to create a monument which would have lasting significance and would be a landmark of our time," an article on nps.gov quotes Saarinen as explaining. "Neither an obelisk nor a rectangular box nor a dome seemed right on this site or for this purpose. But here, at the edge of the Mississippi River, a great arch did seem right."

From 172 entries submitted that summer, five finalists were selected. Initially, the Saarinen family believed the father's design had advanced, celebrating with champagne. Two hours later, when the correction reached the Saarinens, another bottle celebrated the

The Gateway Arch may be America's most photogenic structure.

son's triumph. The following year, Eero Saarinen's design, with an arch now equally tall and wide, won the contest.

Years of engineering and construction lay ahead, and Saarinen died in 1961, a few years before his art soared into the St. Louis sky. Still, he saw his creativity manifested in other famous structures, including airports, universities, and industry. Saarinen's creativity—his art—is preserved in the only national park located in the middle of a city, as well as the only national park that focuses on a human-made structure rather than a natural feature of the landscape.

When walking around the Gateway Arch, it's almost impossible to look away. Every step changes the perspective, the colors, even the sky in the background. Photographers spend hours taking snapshots and never take the same shot twice. Saarinen's art makes an impression, from near or far away.

Architecture, sculpture, painting, photography, music, dance, writing: What art inspires you? How can you use your own artistry and creativity to enrich your life and the lives of others? How can you live to see the art all around you?

GLACIER NATIONAL PARK

MONTANA · 1910 · CONSEQUENCES

*God wasn't at all pleased; but he let them do it their way, worship every new god
that came down the pike—and live with the consequences.*

—ACTS 7:42–43 (MESSAGE)

In Glacier National Park, the only flat surface seems to be the waters of its cold, clear lakes. Jammed with mountains, bisected by a road with astronomical aspirations to match its astral name—Going-to-the-Sun Road—Glacier epitomizes the Rocky Mountains of the American imagination: rugged peaks, narrow valleys, rushing streams, teeming wildlife, and forests broken by green meadows and seasonal wildflowers. Its nickname, Crown of the Continent, is well deserved. Majestic is just one of the words of praise that come to mind for Glacier.

It's hard to imagine North America without the Rocky Mountains, but that's how it looked until about seventy-five million years ago. As the Rockies lifted, an enormous chunk broke off and slid east. The rock in that slab, the Lewis Overthrust, is nearly half a billion years older than the rock that lies beneath it. That same rock lies at the mountainous heart of the park.

Glacier is a place of change in other ways, geological topsy-turvyness aside. The park's western side resembles the rainy Pacific climate. The eastern side is dryer, like the high plains that stretch a thousand miles southeast. Crossing the park latitudinally is almost like driving across the country, but with a better view.

As you look out the car window, you're looking at a relatively new landscape, less than fifteen thousand years old. When you look at the peaks and valleys of Glacier, you see geological breaking news. Many of the valleys were formed in the last great ice age, when glaciers muscled their way down mountains and etched U-shaped gorges between peaks,

A view from Going-to-the-Sun Road

Mount Helen

Wildflowers below Red Eagle Mountain

razor-like ridges when a pair of glaciers shaved a mountain, or sometimes a horn, when three glaciers worked a mountain into a mesmerizing spire.

As the ice retreated, the Blackfeet, Salish, and Kootenai people migrated into the park, living and hunting in the area. As America expanded westward, Glacier's magnificence earned it a hallowed place in the new national park system. Trains delivered the adventurous right to the park's front door. Valleys once unpassable were opened by trails, then by horses and carriages, and finally the engineering marvel that is the Going-to-the-Sun Road, stretching fifty miles across the park and best negotiated by the best white-knuckle driver in the car.

One of the more obvious changes in the park is that the glaciers are disappearing. Glacier National Park was one of the first places to become synonymous with climate change. In recent years, the park recorded three times as many days over ninety degrees than it did a century ago. Snow used to last all summer but is routinely gone by August, and its summers last longer. All that heat is changing the landscape. In 1850, surveyors counted 150 glaciers in the one million acres that eventually became part of the park. Now, there are twenty-six glaciers; almost five of every six glaciers have melted. If climate change continues at its projected rate, Glacier's glaciers will vanish by 2030. Without those glaciers, Glacier's ecosystem will be deeply wounded. Streams will dry up in the summer, leaving the park's natural inhabitants without the water they need. What will Glacier look like in another twenty years?

The human-caused change in Glacier is, without question, appalling. Is there anything we can do? It may be too late to save the glaciers at Glacier, and nobody knows for sure whether climate change has passed the tipping point for the whole planet. Our children and grandchildren may have to figure out how to clean up the mess we made.

There are consequences to the choices we make, whether we want to acknowledge them or not. We think our choices affect only us, but even when we know some choices will have negative consequences, we often choose poorly. Maybe it's leaving your motor idling to keep the air conditioning running, burning more fossil fuel. Maybe it's an addiction. Maybe it's turning a blind eye to injustice or cruelty.

And there are choices that have positive consequences: Making small changes in our habits that will reduce our impact on the world around us. Helping those in need. Standing up for our beliefs and recognizing those who desperately deserve a voice in the conversation yet don't have it.

What unexpected consequence has brought you the most harm? Which brought you the most good? Is there a decision to be made in your life that could make a bigger impact than you expect?

The Flathead River in winter

Blue ice at McBride Glacier

GLACIER BAY NATIONAL PARK

ALASKA • 1980 • CHANGE

Listen, I tell you a mystery: We will not all sleep, but we will all be changed.

—1 CORINTHIANS 15:51 (NIV)

A feature of many national parks is an open geological record marking the passage of time. The walls of the Grand Canyon display millions of years of gradual change as the Colorado River cut its way toward the Baja Peninsula. In the Petrified Forest, fossilized logs lie on the desert floor marking how earth's landscape has changed over time, and we see, extracted from the soil, fossilized remains of creatures that once inhabited the earth. Stands of trees in Redwood, Olympic, Sequoia, Great Basin, and other parks mark time by the passing of hundreds and even thousands of years where they have grown unmoved by their surroundings. In these and other places, we note how *long* it has taken for change to occur.

Glacier Bay National Park is different. Here, change is the main attraction, and it is happening *quickly*. The deck of a cruise ship is the most common platform to watch Margerie Glacier calve off immense chunks of ice into the bay. The accompanying sound, which rangers call "white thunder," occurs as the ice breaks away and meets water. Along with the massive splash and subsequent large waves, you hear a constant chorus of delighted "oohs" and "aahs" from observers. The bay and its shoreline are filled with all of the wildlife you would hope to find within the fields of blue ice and floating icebergs: humpback and killer whales, sea lions, otters, bald eagles, puffins, brown and black bears. It is all framed by steep snow-covered mountains mirrored on the water's surface, which more than doubles its beauty.

What is hard to fathom is that less than 250 years ago, there was no Glacier Bay, at least not in liquid form! The entire sixty-mile trek now taken to reach receding tidewater glaciers from the inlet at Bartlett Cove was covered in ice hundreds of feet thick. As the glaciers advanced, they scoured the landscape of life, cut deep channels in the softer rock, and dragged harder stones with them. Now, as they recede, they melt into the ocean and leave on the land a barren moonscape littered with stony debris.

By the manner in which geologists measure time, this is quicker than lightning! Equally amazing is how swiftly life comes to the desolate ground exposed by the shrinking glacier. Within a year, mosses and lichens grab hold of the rocks to be joined over the next two decades by grasses and wildflowers. Sitka alder and scrub willow follow, and from the decomposition of their leaves, the creation of a hardy soil that allows Sitka spruce to take root, all within the first fifty years after the glacier's retreat. Naturally, animal life follows as the land produces food and shelter. This is remarkably speedy change.

Glacier Bay is more than just the blue walls of ice. Kayaking in the bay, hiking the trails, or simply watching from a ship's deck with a good

Calving glacier

pair of binoculars will yield a more intimate experience with the land and its wild inhabitants. Within the 3.3 million acres, you will find a temperate rain forest and the opportunity to learn about the land's first

Whale "smoke" (breath) from humpback whales

inhabitants, the Huna Tlingit. Totem poles are easy to find and are a staple of the people native to this land, telling the sacred stories and carrying the medicinal and spiritual powers of their beliefs.

"Change is the only constant in life," said the Greek philosopher Heraclitus. We are confronted with change, be it gradual or sudden, in every aspect of life. Some of this change we can direct, and some of it "happens" to us as an outside force. We can fear and dread change, but that won't keep it from coming. When we can be an agent for change and direct it, we need to consider toward what end. Hopefully we do so for the common good. It is best to prepare for change and to manage it as best we can. As glaciers and polar ice are melting at a quickly accelerated pace, scientists express concern about climate change and its impact on the environment. To counter the warming of the globe requires us to change.

How does your faith help you manage the impact of change? How are you an agent of change? How are you making the changes in your carbon footprint necessary to preserve places like Glacier Bay and its wild inhabitants?

The Colorado River continues sculpting the Grand Canyon.

GRAND CANYON NATIONAL PARK

ARIZONA • 1919 • GRANDEUR

Praise the LORD!
I will give thanks to the LORD with my whole heart,
in the company of the upright, in the congregation.
Great are the works of the LORD,
studied by all who delight in them.
Full of honor and majesty is his work,
and his righteousness endures forever.
The fear of the LORD is the beginning of wisdom;
all those who practice it have a good understanding.
His praise endures forever.
—PSALM 111:1–3, 10 (NRSV)

In some places, the Grand Canyon is a mile deep. As the raven flies, from the village on the South Rim to the lodge on the North Rim is less than eleven miles, but it's a 212-mile, nearly five-hour trip by car. Peering across the gorge, top to bottom, you see a geological record spanning nearly two billion years. Two hundred seventy-seven miles of the Colorado River wind through it. The park boundaries protect over 1,900 square miles (1.2 million acres) of ecologically diverse wilderness habitat.

Whether measured by the antlers of the elks who wander its grounds, the Class V-difficulty rapids cascading over boulders in the riverbed, the towering branches of ponderosa pines that line its southern edges, the magic of golden aspen leaves quaking in the barely perceptible autumn breeze in North Rim timber stands, or the wingspans of California condors soaring sublimely in its skies, the life of the park is by any measure big. A *Grand* Canyon indeed!

California Condor resting below Bright Angel Lodge

There are numerous ways to experience the canyon. You can drive along the eastern portion of Desert View Drive, stopping at overlooks along the way, or hop a shuttle bus at the visitor center and choose your stops along the Hermit Road while heading toward Hermit's Rest, the farthest paved access to the west on the South Rim. Hiking the canyon is another option filled with a plethora of choices: the easy Trail of Time, a 1.3-mile paved pathway along the rim embedded with bronze medallions, each signifying a million years of time, or one of many difficult trails that make their way to the floor of the canyon and the river. Riding a mule is another option that can involve a short ride along the North Rim or traversing the gorge rim-to-rim including an overnight stay at Phantom Ranch. If not on foot, by car, or by mule, you can ride the river by boat, gazing at the steep ridges from below rather than above. Some aerial tours are still available, though these have been greatly reduced due to their ecological impact. Even so, that's a lot of options and fitting for a big space to explore.

The North Rim is much more remote and welcomes fewer visitors. Eleven hundred feet higher than the South Rim, it provides different views along with a different ecosystem. Fir trees and aspens replace ponderosa pines and cedars. Here is the only place on earth you will find the tufted-ear Kaibab squirrel (or ghost squirrel).

Despite poetry or prose, photograph or painting, statistics or scale of measure, it is impossible to capture what the canyon is all about. You must see it to believe it. And when you do, you will stand in awe of its grandeur and be humbled at the realization of your own finitude. No one is unmoved by the experience.

An artist encountered early one morning busy with paint and canvas at Point Imperial, the canyon's highest accessible overlook, noted to a passerby: "She doesn't give herself up easily to pen or paper, but that won't keep me from trying to capture how this place speaks to me. I just have to keep coming back, listening, watching, and trying again and again." It is a quest to take ahold of something without fully realizing that it has taken ahold of you, and it won't let you go.

Hermits Rest canyon view

It is not unlike faith—overwhelming, perspective-altering, and difficult to articulate what it feels like to know that the core of your finite being has been touched by

View from Transept Trail, North Rim

the Infinite. When you realize there is something bigger in the universe than you or your issues, it can be both terrifying and oddly reassuring. You could go so far as to say it is "grand."

When in your life has witnessing something "grand" captivated your attention or changed your perspective? When are you particularly awed by the wonder of God as you see it revealed in creation? When you are inspired, what form does your thanksgiving to God take?

GRAND TETON
NATIONAL PARK

Love is patient, love is kind. It does not envy, it does not boast, it is not proud.
It does not dishonor others, it is not self-seeking, it is not easily angered,
it keeps no record of wrongs. Love does not delight in evil but rejoices with
the truth. It always protects, always trusts, always hopes, always perseveres.

—1 CORINTHIANS 13:4–7 (NIV)

You will never see mountains rise so abruptly, so unbelievably, so imposingly, as the Grand Tetons, the forty-mile-long range reaching for the Wyoming heavens. One of the world's youngest ranges, no foothills build up to these mountains. You see only the mountains stretching more than seven thousand feet above Jackson Hole. Once you see the Grand Tetons, you can't take your eyes off them.

As a child, when you drew peaked mountains, you were probably imagining the Grand Tetons. Perfect, snow-capped pyramids, just a single row, with valleys between the peaks and tree-lined alpine lakes at the foot of the range. You'll be amazed to see your drawings come to life.

As at other national parks, glaciers perfected the view you see, but it took a lot of shifting to create the Grand Tetons. Two tectonic plates, sharing a layer of sandstone, collided here, and the eastern plate pushed beneath the western plate. Today, on Skillet Glacier atop Mount Moran is a patch of that reddish sandstone, six thousand feet above the valley. Just to the east, that shared layer of sandstone is now twenty-four thousand feet below ground. Think about a plane flying at an altitude of thirty thousand feet, then imagine huge tectonic plates broken and separated by that same distance! Glaciers chiseled the softer rock around the hard gneiss and granite, revealing the mountains. It's very old rock, but very new mountain.

The Snake River, the Grand Tetons, and the moon

For miles around, the Tetons tower over the landscape. The tallest peak, 13,770 above sea level, is Grand Teton, the park's namesake. It and two neighboring mountains, South Teton and Middle Teton, inspired the name of the Teton Range. Legend has it that in the early 1800s,

Hiking in Death Canyon

Arrowhead balsamroot blooming in the valley below the Grand Tetons

French traders, far from home and perhaps longing for female companionship, named the range *Le Trois Teton*, "the three breasts." Though other names were suggested for the peaks, this name stuck, and the national park's creation—after a ferocious range war with local cattle ranchers that has lasting effects on park management to this date—ended the debate.

Grand Teton is best shared with company, and when the weather is warm, the park offers great hiking, floating, bicycling, fishing, and more. In the winter, you'll likely find no more inspiring place for cross-country skiing. In any season, just a short drive south, Jackson is a classic American tourist town with five-star accommodations, dining, and skiing.

Driving through the park is rewarding in itself, and odds are you will end up near the lakes and streams in Jackson Valley. Many lakes, including Jenny, Bradley, and Taggart, owe their existence to the glaciers, which scooped out lake beds. All around the lakes are moraines, the rocks and sand carved off the mountains that washed downhill in the summer snowmelts or deposited by the glaciers. These lakes and the curvy Snake River provide opportunities for first-time boaters or advanced paddlers to experience the aquatic side of Grand Teton.

Schwabacher Landing on the Snake River

But when mountains are so close, it's hard to ignore their call. Lace up your hiking boots and venture into one of the canyons between the mountains. You may be surprised by the relatively flat trails in the area, particularly those near the lakes. For a challenge, check out Cascade Canyon and the not-as-scary-as-it-sounds Death Canyon. You'll be speechless at the views that reward you when you look out over Jackson Hole or across the valley to the Gros Ventre Mountains. Perhaps you'll have a traveling partner to help you find the words to describe what you're seeing or just to marvel with you.

In the Genesis 2 creation story, God creates the world and then the first human. God quickly realizes that the first human is lonely and creates a second. We know them as Adam and Eve, of course, but the story is truly about human connection and companionship. That story embodies our innate yearning for companionship in our life, having somebody at our side as we journey through life's passes and valleys. They may inspire us to live a better life, offer compassion when we need compassion, the perfect words at the perfect time, or have the ability to salvage a miserable day. Companionship need not take the form that those French trappers had in mind. God created humans to be with other humans, however that relationship presents itself.

Who have been the companions that made your life better? For whom have you been a life-changing companion? How can you be a better companion or friend to a particular person?

Bristlecone pine by starlight

GREAT BASIN NATIONAL PARK

NEVADA • 1986 • ADVERSITY

See, I have refined you, but not like silver;
I have tested you in the furnace of adversity.

—Isaiah 48:10 (NRSV)

Great Basin may well be the grand buffet of national parks. If nature makes it, you can get it here: jagged Wheeler Peak cutting thirteen thousand feet into the sky, Wheeler Glacier continuing to sculpt the land, crystal clear waters rushing over rocks where Bonneville cutthroat trout hide, salt flats from long-departed seas, high desert valleys, subalpine forests. In sizable Lehman Cave, stalactites and stalagmites still reach toward one another, and one of the great "dark sky spots" in North America creating spectacular astronomical viewing. Here you can see the Andromeda galaxy with the naked eye.

In the dry, barren land between the Sierra Nevada and the Wasatch Mountains is a living encyclopedia of harsh forces of the natural world, creating splendor for the human eye to behold. Incredible energies of water, wind, heat, cold, and tectonic movement merge with the sheer will of life to take hold and survive.

The ability to endure in harsh conditions is the story of the park's "must see" resident: the bristlecone pine. At five thousand years old, these trees are among the oldest living things on earth, growing in some of the harshest conditions the planet can offer. Scientists believe it is because of the adverse growing conditions that they are so long-lived.

Is all adversity "bad"? Can you point to a hardship that has made you stronger? Faith does not prevent adversity; how has it helped you to weather it?

GREAT SAND DUNES
NATIONAL PARK

COLORADO • 2004 • MOVEMENT

"Was it because there were no graves in Egypt that you brought us to the desert to die? What have you done to us by bringing us out of Egypt? Didn't we say to you in Egypt, 'Leave us alone; let us serve the Egyptians'? It would have been better for us to serve the Egyptians than to die in the desert!" Moses answered the people, "Do not be afraid. Stand firm and you will see the deliverance the Lord will bring you today. The Egyptians you see today you will never see again. The Lord will fight for you; you need only to be still." Then the Lord said to Moses, "Why are you crying out to me? Tell the Israelites to move on."

—Exodus 14:11–15 (NIV)

The sand dunes are out there, nestled at the end of a valley, pushed up against the towering Sangre de Cristo Mountains. Passing through flat, treeless, scrubby drylands as you work your way north, your eyes may try to tell you that those aren't dunes but the shadow of a cloud or an exposed rock cliff. But when you look carefully, you realize that the graceful tan mounds at the end of the valley are the Great Sand Dunes, the accumulation of thousands of years of the wind's work.

Winds in central Colorado blow from the southwest, eroding tiny pieces of the San Juan Mountains that become blowing sand. But the wind can't carry sand over the towering Sangre de Christos, so staggeringly huge piles of sand pile at the mountain range's base—piles that would reach higher than the tallest buildings in thirty-four states. Pushing in the opposite direction are the winds blowing in from the flat prairies, and rainwater assists in carrying that sand back down into the valley. The sand is pushed back and forth, back and forth, over and over.

The dunes that give Great Sand Dunes National Park its name cover thirty square miles, and the tallest dune is 750 feet tall. Shouldn't that

Cottonwoods, dunes, and Cleveland Peak

number change every time the wind blows? Photos show that while the dunes do change shape, by and large they stay put.

Even when the wind is still, there is movement all around. A single afternoon can bring multiple storms, wind blowing sand into your face and scouring your bare legs, cold rain soaking your clothes. Fifteen minutes later, the sun has dried out your shirt and you're hot again. And you can't see it, but billions of grains of sand just washed downhill or settled as the rain realigned and rearranged the ever-settling dunes. And now more sand, carried in by the storm, is drying and settling into the dunes, while the wind has carried aloft the lightest sand into the sky Maybe it will clear the mountain range, or maybe it will take months or years to roll back downhill.

Take off your shoes and head out to the dunes. Perhaps the sand won't be too hot in the sun; temperatures can reach 150 degrees! On the best days, the fine grains push between your toes but remain firm enough to keep you from sinking in too deeply—at least until you reach the dunes and start climbing. Not quite powdery, you may sink up to your ankles. Running makes your calves ache, and the thin, arid air burns your lungs. For the recreational crowd that wants to stay closer to

Elk at Big Spring Creek

the edge, sandboarding and sandsledding can offer all the fun of a snowy day, minus the heavy insulation and frostbite. Seeing those who have climbed Star Dune, at 750 feet the tallest dune in the park,

Sandhill cranes migrate through the park each spring and fall.

you'll think it looks easy until you've taken a few sandy steps.

When you've decided to head back to the parking lot, you'll need to cross Medano Creek to get back to your campsite or car. When the snow melts, it's a brisk-moving stream intent on reaching the Rio Grande. Most of the year, though, it's shallow enough to provide a cool break and a place to rinse the sand off your feet.

There's more movement at the park if your car is up to the challenge. Beyond the end of the pavement is a road for the most adventurous drivers: twenty-two miles of Medano Road are open for four-wheel drive vehicles, crossing Medano Creek nine times and pushing through four miles of sand.

Atop the sand, in the air, and in the water when it flows, live bighorn sheep, elk, pronghorn, pika, marmots, badgers, and more than 1,500 bison in a nature preserve. More than two hundred species of birds soar the skies over the park, and trout and minnows, frogs, toads, and tiger salamanders ply the waters.

All that movement! Yet it is barely perceptible when we look out at the vast sandy playground of Great Sand Dunes National Park.

Where have you made big moves in your life—geographically, emotionally, or spiritually? What are the moves you want to make and just need to figure out how? How can you help others who seek new ways to live the life God calls them to live?

The Little River in summertime splendor

GREAT SMOKY MOUNTAINS NATIONAL PARK

NORTH CAROLINA AND TENNESSEE
1934 • DIVERSITY

You make springs gush forth in the valleys;
they flow between the hills,
giving drink to every wild animal;
the wild asses quench their thirst.
By the streams the birds of the air have their habitation;
they sing among the branches.
From your lofty abode you water the mountains;
the earth is satisfied with the fruit of your work.
You cause the grass to grow for the cattle,
and plants for people to use,
to bring forth food from the earth,
—PSALM 104:10-15 (NRSV)

The misty haze that often covers high peaks and settles in valleys gives the Great Smoky Mountains their name. Heavily forested hills give off a lot of moisture, and when you couple that with over eighty inches of annual rainfall, you get fog. Most of the pictures you snap (regardless of how clear the day *looks*) will carry the trademark "smoke" that is the namesake of the most visited of all of the national parks.

During a drive along Newfound Gap Road, which traverses the park, elevation ranges from 800 to over 5,500 feet above sea level. Without ever leaving your car, you see wild turkeys and robins scratching under oak trees and ravens soaring above Fraser firs alive with red squirrels.

The park is a study of contrast and diversity. Move through the park from the Blue Ridge Parkway in North Carolina, toward Gatlin-burg, Tennessee, and you go from hundreds of miles of not seeing

Hoar frost covers the forest.

Mingus Mill

a gas station or fast food restaurant to a sudden cacophony of strip-mall style sight and sound. It is as though every pizza parlor and "as seen on TV" store was simply stacked up at the northwest border of the park like pancakes on plate (there are many pancake places too!) awaiting a shot at slaking your thirst for commerce that you were denied along the parkway.

Driving the other direction, you put asphalt and neon in the rearview mirror for the testimony of nature's own wisdom on building a community, with old growth forests and black bears, elk (reintroduced in 2001), and white-tailed deer just wandering about.

Contrasts appear at every turn outside the park and inside: banjo-strumming crooners and singing animated bears in Dollywood. Wood thrushes and waterfalls at the intersection of the Appalachian Trail and the Pigeon River. Plush resorts and thrill-producing roller coasters of suburbia. Water-powered gristmills and the hand-hewn log cabins of the pioneers who settled in the valleys in the nineteenth century. The original inhabitants, the Cherokee, had a smaller footprint, leaving less evidence of how they shared the wonder of this land with its natural inhabitants. It is only a few miles from Gatlinburg's car horns and buffet lines to the sound of dry leaves under your feet and the wind tickling the leaves on the path to Abrams Falls. There is one lodge in the Great Smoky Mountains National Park, reachable only on foot; the lodge is supplied by saddlebag-clad llamas three days a week. It's certainly very different from the hotel in town that sports an entire water park in its lobby!

Even the seasons are incredibly diverse. Spring and fall are beautiful, but for different reasons—one is the beginning of tender green leaves and delicate pastel flowers, the other a seasonal end of those same leaves in fiery reds and bright burning yellows boldly painting the outline of the horizon. Summer's shady canopies hide wildlife in the branches and keep sunlight from the valley floor, whereas winter exposes the framework of the forest's elegant structure and reveals craggy rocks and persistent green growth peeking through the snow, foretelling the miracle of the coming of next spring.

Here, the natural diversity of living things displays the beauty of how difference leads to something wonderful. Driving the park is like looking from a distance at a tapestry that depicts a scene or image. Leaving the car behind to walk the trails and stopping long enough to let the fresh air into your lungs lets you see the individual threads that make the larger image possible. Both views are a wonder. Both are remarkably different. It is all made possible because it is not all the same.

In what ways do you notice and celebrate diversity in your life? How has coming up against something (or someone) different from you made your life richer? How will you help others see the beauty in the diversity of the human family?

View from Clingmans Dome, early autumn

GUADALUPE MOUNTAINS NATIONAL PARK

TEXAS • 1972 • LANDMARKS

The mountain of the LORD's temple will be established as the highest of the mountains; it will be exalted above the hills, and all nations will stream to it.

—ISAIAH 2:2 (NIV)

El Capitan, a towering piece of exposed ocean reef formed from billions and billions of calcium-depositing sponges and algae and ocean mud, is a landmark in the stark, arid western Texas desert. Native Americans, European explorers, and eventually American settlers traveling through looked for the bare, striated rock looming hundreds of feet above the valley. It marks the end of a vast, U-shaped reef, hundreds of miles long, created when the Central Plains were covered in a warm, shallow sea. The Guadalupe Mountains' fossil record includes sea life predating a mass extinction that killed 96 percent of the world's aquatic creatures.

Yet, though a well-known landmark, El Capitan isn't the highest point in the park. That honor goes to Guadalupe Peak. Those who complete the nine-hour hike to the top enjoy a seemingly endless view—or they might take a side trail and head to the top of El Capitan a few miles south.

Our lives have their own landmarks: first steps, first days of school, graduating from high school or college, milestone birthdays, ordinary days that become memorable for reasons we never expected. We eagerly anticipate some landmarks and dread others and even find many bittersweet. We see a date circled on the calendar, get excited or anxious, celebrate it or try to forget it.

What landmarks have you celebrated or dreaded? What landmarks are coming up for you that stir your emotions? What can you do for those who are reaching their own landmarks?

El Capitan

Silversword, found only at Haleakalā Crater

HALEAKALĀ NATIONAL PARK

Now the LORD said to Abram, "Go from your country and your kindred and your father's house to the land that I will show you."

—GENESIS 12:1 (NRSV)

The Hawaiian Islands are 1,800 miles from the North American continent. Whether you sail or fly there, you have to be amazed that anyone in the days of primitive navigation could find them. It's a very small area of land in a vast ocean. As the islands rose from the sea, there were only three ways life could take hold upon the Islands: wind, wave, and wing. Things had to take a journey to get here. Carried by the Pacific currents, blown in on the trade winds, or brought by birds, livings things did, over a long period of time, establish themselves, and the result is a lush tropical paradise.

Most of the island of Maui was formed by the now-dormant volcano at the heart of Haleakalā National Park. Rising nearly two miles above the ocean waves, the landscape still bears lava flows, lava cones, and cinder ash from Haleakalā, which means "home of the sun" in the native language. Lower altitudes are embraced in a tropical rain forest evocative of the Hawaiian paradise of your imagination.

The Polynesians were the first humans carried to the islands by the ocean as they journeyed in their dugout canoes. They arrived sometime between the beginning of the Common Era and the ninth century. There is archeological evidence to show they were using Haleakalā as a site for ceremonies and teaching celestial navigation for use at sea as early as the seventh century. That same evidence suggests several hundred years passed before they inhabited the Kipahulu district along the ocean, also now within the park's borders. It was the summit to

Dried lava flow at Haleakalā Crater

which they journeyed, and if you expend the effort to make the climb as they did, you will discover why.

This is a place where the sunrise and sunsets are so spectacular you literally have to make a reservation to see them! The parking to access this area is limited but planning ahead is worth it. Choose sunrise, and your day will begin in awe and delight. Choose sunset, and you will be treated to an astronomical display unlike many others. After the sun slips below the horizon, under the dark sky you are standing at over ten thousand feet of elevation, adding significant clarity to your view of the cosmos.

Preparation is necessary for your journey up to the summit. As a mountain island in the middle of the Pacific, it can be hot and sunny and cool and rainy all on the same hike. This is backcountry, so there is no cell service. Journey preparations also require water, food, a map, a first-aid kit, and a plan in case of an emergency, as help could be hours away.

This sort of preparation is useful anytime you hike in any of the national parks, and the metaphor certainly carries over into life. When you embark on an intentional journey, you take a limited number of things with you, choosing what to leave behind. Essentials make the trip. Nonessentials do not. The journey begins there, in the choosing. Journeys are made with purpose: a new start, a spiritual awakening, a quest for learning, a change in vocation, joining with a life partner, or becoming a parent. There is a desire to go someplace other than where we are in the present.

Abram and Sarai were called to go on a journey, one for which they could not entirely prepare, save for one thing: they were certain that God had called them to go and would go with them. That was enough. We might say that takes a lot of courage. The Bible said it took a lot faith. It is like the people who took dugout canoes and paddled east into the unknown blue waters of the Pacific. Or when some folks in Palestine decided to follow a rabbi from Nazareth on a very different kind of journey. In both cases, those who went did not remain the same as when they set out.

Haleakalā Crater at sunrise

What kind of journey would you most like to take? In what way would you like to be different than you are now? Is there someone whose company you crave for your journey or would you rather travel alone?

Kuloa Point Trail

HAWAI'I VOLCANOES NATIONAL PARK

HAWAII • 1916 • PARADOX

Where can I go from your spirit?
Or where can I flee from your presence?
If I ascend to heaven, you are there;
if I make my bed in Sheol, you are there.
If I take the wings of the morning
and settle at the farthest limits of the sea,
even there your hand shall lead me
and your right hand shall hold me fast.

—PSALM 139:7–10 (NRSV)

A common expression in real estate is that "they are not making any more land." That is true of most places, but not of Hawai'i Volcanoes National Park. Here, along the Pacific coast, you can see earth just a few years young or, when lava flows freely from Kilauea, only hours old. As molten ground meets the shore and slowly cools, you can watch the "Big Island" grow.

Creating new earth is a smelly and surprisingly loud process with all manner of hissing, popping, and low rumbling of bass shaking the earth, assaulting the nose with the smell of sulfur and hot metals that make the eyes water. Steam screaming to the surface is a toxic cocktail of noxious gases to be avoided for your own safety. When lava moves, everything moves with it. There is no known way to deter it as it slowly, by fire, consumes everything in its path.

To peer into the caldera at Kilauea or at Moku'āweoweo atop Mauna Loa, both active volcanoes within the park, is to imagine the landscape of hell as it might be described by religions and

Halema'uma'u from Jaggar Museum

ancient mythologies that conjure such a home for the damned. Hot mist covers the ground, the lingering smell of ash hangs heavy in the air, and the earth is a blackened, barren, scorched wasteland. The First Testament describes Sheol as a smoldering garbage pit in a valley close to Jerusalem where the shadowy remains of the dead dwell. It could just as easily be here.

Yet despite this place where life seems so absent, living things do encroach at these boundary places. In the middle of the lava field, a single green plant takes hold and defiantly clings to life. Look above the crater's rim and see the verdant vegetation of the tropics. This brutal, inhospitable landscape is the prelude to paradise. Mauna Kea (outside of the park), the highest of the five volcanos that comprise the Big Island, is the tallest mountain on earth, rising thirty thousand feet from the floor of the sea. The South Sea islands we think of as utopia are all products of the same harsh volcanic process—eruption upon eruption, under the waters, until the lava piles high enough upon itself to break above the waves and the ocean's grasp. Life, in a mysterious process, found a way to settle in the cooled lava, and it will eventually do the same here if the mountain again goes dormant. Soil and seeds carried by wind, wave, and creature will make it so.

Hōlei Sea Arch

The trails in the park take you by the sands where endangered hawksbill sea turtles return year after year to lay their eggs and where fish and fowl fill the water and air with life. You can hike up the mountain to listen

Hawai'i Volcanoes moonscape

for the nectar-eating honey creepers twirling among the flowering
trees that dance in the ever-present trade winds, winds that carried the
first living things to these isolated spits of land millennia ago. Gazing
from hill to valley, sea to sky from most any point on your hike, you
may suddenly realize that you never knew there were so many shades of
green and blue in the world.

Take a moment to marvel at the thinness of the margin between
the rust and ochre color of the lava fields and the lush foliage that
surrounds it. From the flaming crucible of the earth's core, life has
formed and taken hold. The space between the two is barely perceptible. The distance between heaven and hell may not be as great as we
suppose. And here, the cycle of life begins in death where the power to
create overcomes the power to destroy. They call it paradise for a reason!

We usually think of death as following life, not the other way around.
What does this park's perspective change for you? Can God dwell in
the thin space between life and death? What assurance or hope does
that give you?

Bathhouse Row and the Arlington Hotel

HOT SPRINGS NATIONAL PARK

ARKANSAS • 1921 • SABBATH

*Remember the sabbath day, and keep it holy. Six days you shall labor and
do all your work. But the seventh day is a sabbath to the LORD your God;
you shall not do any work—you, your son or your daughter,
your male or female slave, your livestock, or the alien resident in your towns.
For in six days the LORD made heaven and earth, the sea, and all that is in them,
but rested the seventh day; therefore the LORD blessed
the sabbath day and consecrated it.*

— EXODUS 20:8–11 (NRSV)

Hot Springs National Park is different from the other parks in
many, many ways. For a start, it's in downtown Hot Springs,
Arkansas, a bustling tourist city in a county with close to one hundred
thousand residents. Parking spots can be hard to find, as can isolation and quiet. It's one of the few parks where the main attractions are
indoors. And it may be the only park where you are encouraged to sit
down, relax, and let your cares wash away.

The western edge of Hot Springs Mountain is riddled with dozens
of springs trickling water that fell as rain four thousand years ago. In
the intervening time, the water has soaked deep into the earth, where it
has been heated by geothermal forces. Each day, half a million gallons
of water surfaces at around 145 degrees—much hotter than tap water,
hot enough to burn skin, but not too hot to scare off intrepid visitors.
For centuries, Native Americans, believing the hot mineral waters could
heal a variety of ailments, visited the site, finding such healing there
that several tribes agreed to share the springs peacefully. Once Europeans settled there, they called for federal protection of the area. Three
years before Arkansas became a state, Congress set aside the land for
future development as a park.

After the Civil War, the popularity of bathhouses soared. Entrepreneurs recognized the opportunity to cash in, and soon a line of rival bathhouses sprang up along Central Avenue, just below the springs. In the 1880s, a dozen bathhouses—the Ozark, the Lamar, the Hale, and more—competed to provide the most attractive services in the most luxurious setting.

Patrons would submerge themselves in the hot waters for a few minutes at a time, followed by rest. Others would sit in metal steam cabinets, their heads poking out the top. Some would submit to stretches using devices that vaguely resemble today's exercise equipment. Eventually, the park superintendent became involved in the regulations for patients, limiting how long showers or baths could be.

While luxurious, the hot springs served a larger audience than the wealthy elite. Indigent and debilitated patients would spend a year or more working with medical professionals in what we would now call physical therapy. In the era of segregation, a separate facility was built for African Americans. Soldiers recovered at the Army and Navy General Hospital overlooking Bathhouse Row.

Hot Springs developed as a resort community and drew its share of famous visitors; entertainers, athletes, gangsters, and politicians all visited the area during its heyday. But eventually the bathing fad faded, and many of the bathhouses closed. In recent years, though, a renaissance has sparked new energy in Hot Springs. Two buildings reopened as spas, another as an art museum, and the National Park Service uses the former Fordyce Bathhouse as a visitor center and history museum.

Hot Springs from West
Mountain Trail

If you take advantage of the spas, you'll feel quite different in just a few hours. In the solitude of a private room, you can soak away your concerns in a mineral bath. A masseuse will work on those tight muscles and ease away the stress you bring with you. The heat of the water or the steam

Stained glass inside the Fordyce, a spa converted to a museum

room loosens your muscles and your mind. With a staff that dotes on you but also gives you space to be comfortable, you can get a break from the grind and pressure of twenty-first-century life.

When you're not at the springs, you may find yourself ready for a hike. Bathhouse Row is nestled between two mountains; both offer trails with broad views of the Hot Springs area. Oak, hickory, and pines blanket the hillsides; many of them are more than 130 years old. In a busy park, animals can be rare, but you will be sharing a forest with deer, turkey, squirrels, rabbits, armadillos, and—be careful!—skunks and snakes.

We often think of the outdoors as a place to "get away from it all," to calm down and catch our breath. We need that break. The idea of sabbath—one day a week to focus on what really matters, to reflect and to rest and to find peace— is often lost in our culture. Reclaiming that holy time sure seems like a good idea, doesn't it?

What have you found to be the most effective ways to relax? Do you relax often enough for your own good? How can you help others find the break and peace they need?

Porch of the Quapaw bathhouse

On a clear day, the Chicago skyline peeks over the Lake Michigan horizon.

INDIANA DUNES NATIONAL PARK

INDIANA • 2019 • COMPROMISE

We who are strong ought to bear with the failings of the weak and not to please ourselves. Each of us should please our neighbors for their good, to build them up.

— ROMANS 15: 1–2 (NIV)

A fifteen-mile-long ribbon of parkland along Lake Michigan, Indiana Dunes is a patchwork of sand dunes, swamps, marshes, bogs, forests, prairies, and savanna threading between neighborhoods, steel mills, transportation arteries, and a busy shipping port.

In this tight space are ten different habitats, created by retreating glacial ices that left behind the sand that comprises the park's best-known feature and differentiated by the animals and plants that thrive there. Industrial construction largely eradicated the dune and swale habitat, but other remaining ecosystems testify to the tension between preservation and industrialization. The land—sweeping vistas, unique habitats, and historical landmarks—and its inhabitants—snail darters, spotted owls, and bald eagles—have often competed to claim their own value in the face of economic progress, community development, and job creation.

At our best, we steward resources to preserve claims of competing forces. We compromise so the best of each can go forward in harmony rather than enmity. Ironically, Indiana Dunes reflects that balance not only in its terrestrial composition but in its birth: the congressional spending bill creating the park was itself a political compromise to avoid a government shutdown.

Our lives are filled navigating such tensions. The biblical challenge seems to be, What is the best way to find a "win-win" scenario? We are called to love not just ourselves nor our neighbors exclusively, but both.

When has compromise solved a stalemate? When do you hold your ground? What makes the difference in choosing one over the other?

ISLE ROYALE NATIONAL PARK

MICHIGAN • 1940 • ISOLATION

The one who lives alone is self-indulgent,
showing contempt for all who have sound judgment.

— PROVERBS 18:1 (NRSV)

D o you ever fantasize about escaping to a remote island? For all the meaning and joy they bring us, the pressures of responsibilities and relationships are, at times, simply overwhelming. National parks are a good antidote for this, and Isle Royale, tucked away in the cold waters of western Lake Superior, may be just the spot to enjoy some time away. It qualifies as secluded, for it is accessible only by boat or plane. The park headcount reveals that not many people go there; your daytime activities are limited to hiking, boating, watching wildlife, or being alone with your thoughts in beautiful surroundings. It's an introvert's dream!

The problem with being on an island is that while isolation can be attractive, over the long haul it also has it problems, as the writer of Proverbs knew. Isle Royale is the location of an ongoing study of the relationship between predator (wolves) and prey (moose) that includes how a constantly shifting balance between the two impacts the environment, and the effect of a limited gene pool on breeding and sustainability. The smaller wolf population has declined significantly since first appearing on the island, and a specific spinal deformity amplified by limited breeding stock is partly to blame.

Isolation, despite some benefits, has its limitations.

How do you find balance between isolation and engagement? How are some people isolated by factors other than their own choice? How does cultural isolation diminish us as a community?

A young bull moose takes a postwinter bath.

Joshua tree at sunset

JOSHUA TREE NATIONAL PARK

CALIFORNIA • 1994 • ADAPTATION

[F]or I have learned to be content whatever the circumstances. I know what it is to be in need, and I know what it is to have plenty. I have learned the secret of being content in any and every situation, whether well fed or hungry, whether living in plenty or in want. I can do all this through him who gives me strength.

—PHILIPPIANS 4:11–13 (NIV)

It's a miracle that anything can live out there at all. With sandy soil baked in the summer heat, barely any rain, and no streams bringing water from elsewhere, at first glance Joshua Tree National Park seems like one of the most barren places imaginable.

A few hours away from the bustle of Los Angeles, Joshua Tree is tucked behind the Little San Bernadino Mountains, far enough inland that any Pacific breezes blowing in have had their moisture drained out of them. During the summertime, highs are usually in the triple digits, and nights still stay warmer than you set your air conditioner at home. Cooler seasons bring cooler weather, but there's a reason the Palm Springs area, on the southern side of the mountains, is so attractive to "snowbirds" avoiding the much more intense winters in other parts of North America. For while it snows occasionally in Joshua Tree, it's rarely cold.

Joshua Tree encompasses two different deserts, which may seem a bit odd. Deserts are deserts, right? But when you look more closely, you see the difference.

The Mojave Desert, the western half of the park, is largely above three thousand feet in elevation, making it a bit cooler. In this sandy, rocky space thrives the Joshua tree, christened by Mormons seeking a new homeland and remembering a kindred homeland-seeking ancestor in Joshua. The Mormons envisioned Joshua reaching skyward,

Cholla cactus

Ocotillo cactus

imploring God for guidance just like the spindly plant. Unique to the Mojave and found mostly in California, Nevada, and Arizona, Joshua trees are different from the trees you'll find in your local park. Because they're not covered in leaves, the unusual limb structures are mesmerizing. They're also photogenic, because no two Joshua trees appear to grow the same way.

Joshua trees are a variety of yucca with thick branches coated in what looks like furry bark. Spiky evergreen leaves sprout at the branches' ends, reducing the water lost to evaporation. After a new tree survives its first freeze, it blooms with cream-colored flowers in the spring, followed by an edible fruit. Instead of adding a ring each year, Joshua tree trunks are fibrous, which makes it hard to tell exactly how old the trees are. However, trees can live for hundreds of years, and a few have survived a thousand. Fast growers for deserts, adding about an inch-and-a-half each year, Joshua trees can reach fifty feet in height; that their roots dig almost as deep helps them find whatever moisture comes along.

As durable as they are, climate change threatens their long-term survival. A 2001 study suggests that their range will be reduced 90 percent by the end of the century, and perhaps be entirely wiped out in its namesake park. Can the Joshua tree adapt to that change so quickly? Nobody knows.

As you travel east through the park, you also go downhill and descend into the Colorado Desert, which is largely below three thousand feet in elevation. Encompassing the eastern half of the park, the Colorado is dryer and hotter—on average eleven degrees hotter—than the Mojave. That habitat has created a different ecosystem, with different plants that can tolerate the even more hostile climate. Gone are the Joshua trees; here, the plants are scrubbier and smaller. Lucky visitors can see cholla cacti and their bright yellow flowers, protected inside by spiky needles. Those lucky visitors, though, can find themselves plucking out spines if they get too close; cholla are also called "jumping cholla" because of their ability to attach themselves to visitors and hitch a ride to a new location.

The animals living in the park have also adapted to survive: by burrowing out of reach of the sun, by changing their biology to use water more efficiently, or by being primarily nocturnal. When the sun sets, the bighorn sheep, coyotes, lynx, black-tailed rabbits, and reptiles like lizards and snakes emerge from hiding.

As inhospitable as the park seems, miners and ranchers have attempted to live in the desert, with some success. Silver and gold worth about $5 million in today's terms was extracted from the ground here. Later, Bill and Frances Keys lived for six decades in the park, and visitors can tour their homestead—a testament to surviving and thriving in less-than-ideal situations.

Joshua Tree National Park is a living monument to adaption and figuring out how to deal with a challenging, seemingly unavoidable situation. What challenges have forced you to adapt to new circumstances? What has helped you adapt when you knew that change wouldn't be easy? What talents do you have to help others adapt to unexpected change?

Streaked clouds over the desert

KATMAI NATIONAL PARK

ALASKA • 1980 • JOY

The pastures of the wilderness overflow,
the hills gird themselves with joy,
the meadows clothe themselves with flocks,
the valleys deck themselves with grain,
they shout and sing together for joy.
—PSALM 65:12–13 (NRSV)

Katmai National Park is not near the top of a list of quickly recognized national parks. But the indelible images from Katmai are ubiquitous, recognized by anyone who has seen a nature documentary: bears . . . lots of brown bears eating lots of sockeye salmon in the Alagnak River at Brooks Falls. In the mid-to-late summer, they gather along the shore to gorge themselves on the fish, to play in the rushing water, and to fight for dominance in the quest to acquire a mate. It is a thrilling display, and it draws tourists who come by boat or float plane.

Before you can see the bears, however, you *must* view a ranger-led program about bear safety. Bears are fun to watch, but they are still inherently dangerous and unpredictable. That edge of excitement and danger adds to the joy of watching them.

A great many things that are worth doing, seeing, or experiencing are filled with joy precisely because they have an edge of excitement: sightseeing in the wilderness, riding a roller coaster, or falling in love are just a few examples,

What brings you joy? Could your faith use a little more joy *and* excitement? What might that look like?

Fishing at Brooks Falls

Holgate Glacier calving

KENAI FJORDS NATIONAL PARK

ALASKA • 1980 • SIGNS

He answered them, "When it is evening, you say, 'It will be fair weather,
for the sky is red.' And in the morning, 'It will be stormy today, for the sky is red
and threatening.' You know how to interpret the appearance of the sky,
but you cannot interpret the signs of the times.

— MATTHEW 16:2–3 (NRSV)

Kenai Fjords is the smallest of the Alaskan national parks, but it contains the largest icefield that is solely within the United States. At over seven hundred square miles, the Harding Icefield feeds thirty-five glaciers, many of which sculpted the deep fjords and inlets along the Gulf of Alaska coast. In the far eastern section of the park, Exit Glacier is the only glacier you can drive to observe. Along the road to Exit View are numbered signs that may appear to be mile markers; these numbers are actually dates, and their locations mark the glacier's terminus over the last two centuries. The signs indicate that the glacier is rapidly retreating.

Other glaciers in the park are tidewater glaciers, meaning that their terminus is the ocean. As they calve into the fjords, they create a unique ecosystem. When the massive chunks of ice tumble into the water, they churn up nutrients from below, attracting fish, birds, and mammals. The food chain is in clear sight: from the plankton and small fish that feed upon them to the bald eagle and humpback whale who likewise feed on them! Sea lions, otters, puffins, peregrine falcons, and the ever-present seagulls work over and under the surface in constant search for their prey. To experience these spectacles you will need a boat, and the signs will point you to numerous outfitters and concessionaires.

Aside from the observation point for Exit Glacier, there are ways to experience the park by land. The Harding Icefield Trail climbs four

Breaching humpback whale

thousand feet in elevation from Exit Glacier and offers extraordinary views. Cabins and camps within the park can be accessed by boat or float plane. Know they are rustic and that you need to bring your own camping gear. Know too that mosquitoes also love the park—and its visitors! A respite here will give you a chance to see bears, mountain goats, and the beautiful vegetation that overtakes the barren land left behind by a retreating glacier. Most people see the park from the water, but experiencing it from the land is equally amazing; the beauty is arresting. Archeologists have found signs that Sugpiaq people have been in the fjords harvesting its resources and enjoying its splendor for a thousand years.

You cannot visit here without learning something about global climate change. Kenai Fjords and the Harding Ice Field are among the places where intense research is documenting the changes that are occurring. Scientists refer to Alaska as the "crystal ball" of climate science, as the impact of the earth's warming is being seen and felt here ahead of many other places on the planet. In itself, marking the increased rate at which ice is melting does not tell us why, but it does demonstrate that the planet is getting warmer. Shrinking ice is a compounding problem: the more ice disappears, the less sunlight reflects back into space, which means more warmth is absorbed back into the oceans and the land, which increases the rate of warming . . . which further shrinks the ice and adds additional warmth. It is called a feedback loop. Is it a sign?

In the Bible, signs matter. Abundance at harvest, a sign of blessing; locusts consuming the crops, Divine displeasure. To us, this is the worldview of a prescientific culture. Yet, the people of those cultures understood signs as symptoms and even forecasts. Failure to pay attention to justice can lead to civil unrest. A breakdown in community bonds might be the result of acts of untruthfulness, taking what doesn't belong to you, unfaithfulness in intimate relationships, or valuing your neighbor's stuff more than your neighbor. To continue in such a way is to risk disaster.

But some signs are even hopeful. A baby is born in a stable in Bethlehem, and some shepherds took it as a sign that God, no matter what, has chosen to be with us.

How do you pay attention to signs? What signs concern you? What signs give you hope?

Sea otter

KINGS CANYON NATIONAL PARK

CALIFORNIA • 1940 • MISSION

[Jesus] said to them, "Go into all the world and preach the gospel to all creation."
— MARK 16:15 (NIV)

The flooding of Yosemite National Park's Hetch Hetchy Valley is often cited as the beginning of America's environmental movement. One hundred miles southeast, Kings Canyon National Park reigns as one of the movement's most remarkable successes.

Best known as the deep gorge of the Kings River, the valley languished for years in the arboreal shadow of neighboring Sequoia, the second national park. The gorge and the remote wilderness farther up the Kings River valley were difficult to access, and roads were slow to reach the valley.

Meanwhile, Los Angeles got thirsty. The growing metropolis 180 miles south craved fresh water. Los Angeles looked north to the Sierra Nevada Mountains, just as San Francisco had looked to Hetch Hetchy in the northern expanses of Yosemite. There, after years of legal battles, protests, and eventually federal action, the O'Shaughnessy Dam flooded the Hetch Hetchy Valley in 1923. While San Francisco gained hydroelectric power and a more stable water supply, America lost what John Muir compared to "cathedrals and churches"—holy ground.

Dropping eleven thousand feet in less than eighty miles, Kings Canyon has all the makings of a great hydroelectric dam site. Developers drooled over possibilities while environmental groups pressured Congress to create a national park. For years the two sides were mired in a stalemate. In the meantime, highway construction scraped through difficult terrain toward the valley, and trails proliferated in the wilderness. Small improvements were made by the U.S. Forest Service, but larger ones were deterred by the prospect of a dam flooding the valley.

Zumwalt Meadows

McClure Meadow

Eventually, Interior Secretary Harold Ickes saw the opportunity to end the debate once and for all. A strong proponent of the park, he rallied local support and hired respected nature photographer Ansel Adams to photograph the valley. Adams's photos and public support finally earned national park status for Kings Canyon in 1940.

But Kings Canyon wasn't out of the woods yet. Eight years later, Los Angeles again applied to construct dams, and the federal government rejected the applications. This application-and-denial cycle continued until 1963. Those lawsuits have ended, but a quiet reminder remains: The U.S. Forest Service, not the National Park Service, manages the area between the Kings River Canyon and the small cluster of sequoia trees in Grants Grove, meaning it could be tapped for water someday. The parched-but-growing Desert Southwest could once again look to Kings Canyon.

Elsewhere in the park, another scar of environmental abuse continues healing. In the Big Stump Grove, loggers devastated hundreds of sequoia. While the grove shows signs of recovery, it will take hundreds, perhaps thousands, of years until a visitor will no longer notice the damage humans inflicted. Big Stump's location near the park entrance may serve as a reminder to treasure God's gifts today and to be good stewards of those gifts so we can pass them along to generations to come.

Today, what Muir called "a yet grander valley" than Yosemite is a hiker's paradise. Beyond the single finger-like road following the river, it is mostly wilderness. Between geologically young granite walls reaching up thousands of feet, carved by glaciers descending from the tallest mountains in the contiguous United States, lies the fast-rushing river and, in wider expanses, the Zumwalt Meadow blanketed in grass. Glaciers, tarns, and hanging valleys—and silence—welcome hikers to the higher, distant reaches.

Many, like Muir, have discovered the conservation of America's wild spaces as their mission in life, and national parks often served as the setting and inspiration for those epiphanies. Their environmental mission continues in many ways: combating climate change, creating green space in local communities, recycling trash, energy conservation, and creating mass transit, to name a few. There are so many worthwhile pursuits: antiracism, antipoverty, literacy, education, public safety, criminal justice reform, the list goes on and on. We belong to organizations like churches or civic groups that have their own unique missions. When we have a common cause, a mission, that unites us, we find the courage to face difficult challenges. We may also find we succeed.

What missions have energized you in the past? What missions are you considering for the next few years of your life? How can you help others discover and engage in missions of their own?

Tokopah Falls

KOBUK VALLEY NATIONAL PARK

ALASKA • 1980 • SUSTENANCE

There on the wilderness ground was a fine flaky something, fine as frost on the ground…. Moses told them, "It's the bread GOD has given you to eat."
—EXODUS 16:13–16 (MESSAGE)

For at least nine thousand years, the Inupiat have lived and died by what happened in the landscape we now call Kobuk Valley National Park. Tucked away in Alaska's northwestern reaches, Kobuk Valley is where caribou herds cross the Kobuk River and encounter towering sand dunes. The Inupiat knew that the river and dunes provided excellent caribou hunting grounds and that the river gave salmon. Without nature's movement providing the opportunity to hunt, this land would have been uninhabitable. The Inupiat used the gifts wisely.

Kobuk Valley is known mostly for its dunes, the result of repeated glaciation that ground the rocks into sand. Prevailing easterly winds and glacial runoff created three dune fields that once covered more than three hundred square miles. In the centuries since, the forest and tundra have reclaimed about 90 percent of that area, but the dunes remain—and are now even more impressive, given how out of place sand dunes look in the icy northern reaches of the world.

A place of extremes, winter temperatures in the Kobuk Valley plummet to -50 degrees Fahrenheit and rocket to triple digits in the summertime. Because it's north of the Arctic Circle, when the sun finally rises in early June it doesn't set for more than a month. Kobuk Valley is hard to reach; with no roads, the best way to reach the park—once you fly in on a small airplane—is to float the sixty-one miles of the Kobuk River within the park.

What sustains you in hard times? Where have you seen gifts that others overlook? How can you be better at sustaining others?

Caribou cross the Kobuk River.

LAKE CLARK NATIONAL PARK AND PRESERVE

ALASKA • 1980 • SOLITUDE

As John's disciples were leaving,
Jesus began to speak to the crowd about John:
"What did you go out into the wilderness to see?"
—MATTHEW 11:7 (NIV)

It's easy to be alone at Lake Clark National Park. Accessible only by boat or plane, it is one of the least visited national parks. Mountainous, laced with protected rivers and lakes, the park is best known for Mount Redoubt, an active volcano that last erupted in 2009, and for the nature of Alaskan lore: grizzly and black bears, moose and caribou, puffins and eagles, salmon, and blueberries and cranberries.

Without extensive development or well-marked trails, exploring on your own requires backcountry hiking experience and survival skills. Glaciers continue gouging the landscape, filling three wild and scenic rivers that provide extended floating opportunities through challenging rapids. As you explore Lake Clark, the occasional plane passing overhead may be the only other human activity you see.

Solitude, of course, can be a good thing if you're wanting to get away from the busyness and noise of daily life. Everybody needs to get away from the routine, to find time to focus, to remember what matters in life, simply to breathe. While national parks can be crowded and hectic, each of them provides a way to escape the crowds, though you may have to look carefully to find those opportunities.

When you need to get away, what places do you crave? How do you help others find time in their lives to make their own wilderness? How can you create needed solitude in the midst of your home or work?

Redoubt Volcano from Crescent Lake

Lassen Peak and Kings Creek

LASSEN VOLCANIC
NATIONAL PARK

CALIFORNIA • 1916 • POTENTIAL

I can do all things through [the one] who strengthens me.

—Philippians 4:13 (NRSV)

If you're a person of a certain age, you remember Mount St. Helens's gigantic eruption in 1980. Those a few generations back remember Lassen Peak.

Native Americans knew Lassen Peak was unstable and named it *Amblu Kai*, "Mountain Ripped Apart." Archeologists find little evidence of human settlement in the area, and geologists estimate that the previous eruption occurred (relatively speaking) not long ago, around 1666. That eruption ripped a crater 360 feet deep and 1000 feet across the summit. Later, American settlers told stories of fire in the sky, but the volcano was widely viewed as dormant despite several indicators of volcanic activity in the area. Lassen Peak and Cinder Cone, both volcanic in origin, were protected as national monuments in 1907.

Apparently, Lassen Peak decided to take things a step further. On May 30, 1914, the volcano rumbled back to life when a steam vent blasted a hole in the mountain, and the hole became a deep lake. Over the next year, the mountain kept steaming, the lake kept growing, and the world watched, wondering what would happen.

A year later, activity took off. Eruptions propelled lava chunks up to twenty miles away, and a lava dome swelled up inside the crater. Five days later, another eruption destroyed that dome, leaving a new crater and creating a mudslide half a mile wide and four miles long that flooded more than thirty miles of Hat Creek and the Pit River. And the world waited to see what would happen next.

On the afternoon of May 22, a Saturday, Lassen Peak exploded, creating a plume of ash and gas that reached thirty thousand feet into the skies. A lahar, or volcanic mudflow, stretched fifteen miles from the volcano, destroying three square miles of forest that still bears the name "The Devastated Area." Ash from the volcano blew into Nevada. Though not as intense as Mount St. Helens would be, it was still notable.

Lassen Peak continued steaming and rumbling for another seven years, but eventually the volcano settled down. In its seven-year run, about four hundred eruptions were noted. It would be six decades until another mountain in the Cascades erupted in Washington.

Don't let its silence fool you: Lassen Peak is still an active volcano. When you stand on the back patio of the visitor center, you stare into the rocky maw of an ancient volcano. Mount Tehama once stood a thousand feet taller than Lassen does now, but eruptions, combined with the collapse of its magma chamber and rocks chemically weakened by the acid emitted in volcanic vapors, left a bowl-shaped caldera two miles across. Brokeoff Mountain, Mount Conrad, Mount Diller, and Pilot Pinnacle circle the caldera, reminders of what once was.

Fumaroles, mud pots, hot springs, and geysers dot the park and give amateur volcanologists a chance to examine the earth's inner workings up close. Down the road from the visitor center lie Sulphur Works, Devils Kitchen, Boiling Springs Lake, and Bumpass Hell, named for a local resident who survived stumbling into the scalding water. These days, Lassen Volcanic is a beautiful recovering landscape, including The Devastated Area.

Who knows whether Lassen Peak will erupt again? Potential volcanoes stretch from California to Alaska. All it takes is the right circumstances—a weak spot in the earth's crust and a hot spot just below—to bring Lassen, or any old volcano or volcano-in-waiting back to life. There's no telling what might happen.

That's the thing about potential: it's hard to predict. Potential can be inspiring—"she has so much potential! She's going to do great things!"—or devastating—"This has the potential to go very, very wrong." Our all-loving God prefers the inspiring route, right? Why else would God have created us to experience love and joy and happiness and delight and curiosity and intelligence? We humans are built to think about what might be.

We make many decisions based on our life experiences, our education, and our practical knowledge. But there are some decisions we have to make without the benefit of that practical knowledge. We predict various outcomes, take an educated guess as to which will yield the best result, and get to work. We make those decisions on potential, asking, "How can I make the most of this opportunity?"

Who or what helped you see your potential at different times in your life? Where do you see potential working in your life, or where is it untapped? How can you help somebody else release their own potential?

Boiling Springs Lake

MAMMOTH CAVE NATIONAL PARK

KENTUCKY • 1941 • DARKNESS

Where can I go from your Spirit?

Where can I flee from your presence?

If I go up to the heavens, you are there;

if I make my bed in the depths, you are there. . . .

If I say, "Surely the darkness will hide me,

and the light become night around me,"

even the darkness will not be dark to you;

the night will shine like the day,

for darkness is as light to you.

—PSALM 139:7-8, 11–12 (NIV)

As the name implies, Mammoth Cave is big! Contrary to what some might expect, and despite sharing a name with the prehistoric elephant-like creatures, there are no known wooly mammoth fossils in it. This park is really two very different parks: one underground, the other above. Above, eight-five square miles of forest and hillsides feature trails for hikers, mountain bikers, and equestrians. The Green River meanders through the park and is a favorite spot for kayakers and canoers, with anglers hugging the banks at the lower section of the river in search of small mouth bass and other sport fish. Not all that long ago, the Green was so polluted by untreated sewage, coal ash, PCBs, and farm chemical run-off that it was unfit for recreational use. Now eighty species of fish, fifty species of mussels, and an abundance of winged, walking, and crawling wildlife shares the space with human visitors to the park. It is one of many testimonials to the beneficial work of conservation and protection.

Despite the splendor found hiking in the daylight or camping under the stars, the main attraction is a portion of the more than

Domes & Dripstones Tour

Kayaking the Green River

four hundred mapped miles of underground passages that comprise the largest known cave system on earth. Don't feel overwhelmed, though: only about twelve miles of passages are open to the public. The cave was formed from the remnants of a once-shallow tropical sea that left behind sediment that became rock. Underground rivers then carved through that rock. Rangers will tell you about the geological record if you are interested, but most people are fascinated by how the cave is now—"now," of course being relative, encompassing the last five thousand years or so of activity from which there is evidence of how the cave has been used and experienced from a human perspective.

Not only is the cave large, its "landscape" is incredibly diverse. The tour selections are as distinct as the various regions of the cavernous network of connecting spaces. A vaulted ceiling that soars 192 feet overhead at Mammoth Dome is quite a contrast to the spots that are too narrow to fit through if you are more than forty-two inches across (Fat Man's Misery). Only a few sections of this cave have the formations of stalactites and stalagmites you might expect to find.

Despite the cave's rugged beauty and a human history of use that encompasses everything from mining salt and gypsum to serving as a hospital for tuberculosis patients, there is one amazing thing that stands over against the others: its darkness. Complete and utter darkness.

Turn out the lights, extinguish your lantern flame or any sort of portable illumination, and you are at once plunged into it. Such total darkness is incredibly disorienting. A moment ago, you could see where you were in relation to everything and everyone else. Now you are immersed in the inky blackness, with no sense of where the people, the walls, the ceiling, or even the cave floor are in the space you occupy. It freezes you in place. You may want to move, but you can't.

This total absence of light creates instant anxiety. You can sense it in the people you can no longer see around you. There is a sensation of "being swallowed up" by the sudden void of light. You are instantly and hopelessly lost. You can attempt to comprehend it, taking deep breaths, seeking to find a centering point in the moment. You have likely never experienced a blackness this deep. The rangers don't let you stay that way too long. But in that darkness, when you can focus on nothing in your surroundings save the cool air and the silence of the space, something is different. The darkness isolates you from everything but yourself.

Then, with the striking of a match, you see how true it is that it takes very little light to overcome immense darkness.

In your life, have you had a sense of being so completely lost that you believed even God could not find you? Who or what has been light to shatter a darkness you have experienced? In what ways are you being light to shatter the darkness of others?

Broadway in Mammoth Cave

Cliff Palace

MESA VERDE NATIONAL PARK

Above all, love each other deeply, because love covers over a multitude of sins.
Offer hospitality to one another without grumbling.
Each of you should use whatever gift you have received to serve others,
as faithful stewards of God's grace in its various forms.

—1 PETER 4:8–10 (NIV)

Fifteen hundred years ago, a nomadic Native American tribe decided instead to stay put, settling into a canyon-rutted plateau near the Four Corners where Colorado, Utah, New Mexico and Arizona meet. They created small communities, building "pithouses," homes dug a few feet into the ground with a simple hole in the roof for ventilation. In that not-so-simple act of settling down, the Puebloans, named for the Spanish word for *town*, changed their way of life by taking up farming and by taking advantage of a new technology: bows and arrows. Over the course of several hundred years, their simple huts incorporated stone masonry, and their elaborate structures, some with more than fifty rooms, sprung up on the plateau. Occasionally, a bold builder ventured into the nearby cliff walls.

For the next seven centuries, Puebloan architecture evolved into magnificent, sturdy buildings clustered into villages. Pithouses evolved into *kivas*, excavated enclosed chambers used for ceremonies and as community gathering spaces, much like today's churches. Puebloans entered kivas by descending a ladder through a hole in the roof, symbolic of an entrance to the underworld.

These homes suited them for a while, but it is their achievements in their final century in the area that make Mesa Verde particularly unforgettable.

In the twelfth century, the Puebloans constructed magnificent cities tucked into the canyon wall crevices. Nestled amid the weather-beaten rocks and the canyon floor, below rock faces that sheltered them from the harsh winters and broiling summers, they built a city on the cliff—taupe sandstone buildings, bricks the size of shoeboxes cemented together with mortar of mud—a city that defied gravity and boggled the most creative imagination.

Why the Puebloans retreated to the cliffs is unknown, but for a while it was a wise move. Several thousand people lived in the cliff-side homes, and the city thrived. Today visitors to the pueblos get an intimate glimpse at life in what was surely a tightly knit community. By today's standards, many rooms are small and cramped—a six-foot by eight-foot room would have housed three people. Several generations shared a structure, adding rooms as the clan grew. In the sparsely populated and often inhospitable terrain of the American Southwest, families and clans stayed together for a lifetime.

It's easy to imagine the bustling community. Farmers brought food into the village from family plots in the valley. Others stayed in the village, producing pottery and baskets, sandals and hunting tools, working with leather and fabrics, satisfying the everyday needs of the community. Mesa Verde had a shared economy, and their productivity enabled them to trade even with distant neighbors; in fact, artifacts from across North America have been unearthed at Mesa Verde.

And then, in the course of just a few generations, Mesa Verde was abandoned, but we don't know why. Was it because of drought, exhausted natural resources, or warfare? Whatever the cause, by the late thirteenth century, the Puebloans had dispersed. Today, 750 years later, about two dozen tribes trace their lineage back to the Puebloans, and similar architecture and cliff dwellings dot the Southwest.

Long forgotten or overlooked, the ruins were rediscovered in the 1880s. Within a few decades, Mesa Verde was among the first national parks.

Today, visitors walk through the hallowed alleys of the ancient cities, still marveling at the craft, ingenuity, and artistry evident in the sturdy structures where babies were born, elders died, and the community lived with the same joys and griefs we feel today. Descending the trail from the visitor center into the valley, then ascending ladders to peek into what once was a family home, we get hints of what life was like in this unlikely village. Tours of Cliff Palace, Spruce Tree House, and Balcony House, as well as the more than four thousand identified sites, transport us out of our own time in ways unlike any other national park.

But at Mesa Verde, we do more than time-travel. We see another way of life in which the connections that linked individuals into communities were far more evident. When a child was born, everybody celebrated. When the crops failed, everybody went hungry. When warfare erupted, the entire community sacrificed. When the way of life collapsed, the community dispersed. Mesa Verde helps us to see the community we may not always recognize around us.

What communities have sustained and nurtured you over the course of your life? What communities have helped you through the hardest times and the most joyous celebrations? How can you contribute more to the communities you hold close to your heart?

Spruce Tree House in winter

MOUNT RAINIER NATIONAL PARK

WASHINGTON • 1899 • REVELATION

Moses said, "Show me your glory, I pray." And he said, "I will make all my
goodness pass before you, and will proclaim before you the name, 'The LORD';
and I will be gracious to whom I will be gracious, and will show mercy on whom
I will show mercy. But," he said, "you cannot see my face;
for no one shall see me and live."

—Exodus 33:18–20 (NRSV)

Mount Rainier is a truly iconic symbol of the northwestern United States. At over 14,400 feet, it is the tallest mountain in the Cascades, and when Rainier is "out," you can see it for a hundred miles from every point on the compass. Continuously changing cloud formations hide, then reveal, the mountain and alter its appearance in an ongoing game of peek-a-boo.

It is also an active volcano. Were it to erupt, which it has done as recently as the 1890s, eighty thousand-plus homes around the cities of Tacoma and Seattle would be vulnerable. Frequent calving of glaciers, avalanches, mudflows (called lahars), and landslides destroy hiking trails and fill in valleys. It is a wild area, with bears and mountain lions, sudden blizzards, unexpected dense fog, outburst floods, and debris flows. Park information pointedly states that if you hear a loud boom or continued "rumbling," you should seek higher ground immediately! Its untamed beauty makes it potentially dangerous, yet its allure is powerful.

The mountain's size should not be underestimated. It holds two dozen glaciers, four dozen permanent snowfields, hundreds of lakes, acres of wetlands and marshes, and impressive waterfalls. It serves as the headwaters for several major rivers including the Puyallup, Mowich, White, Carbon, and Kautz. Fragile meadows explode into a technicolor ocean

Rainier above the clouds

Relfections from a small lake in the Tatoosh mountain range

of wildflowers in the briefest of seasons between snowmelt and snowfall.

Stop at the Grove of Patriarchs and hike 1.5 miles into the old-growth forest and dwell with trees that were saplings when William the Conqueror invaded England in 1066. Try for a moment to comprehend what those trees have witnessed as the earth has ventured around the sun a thousand times, and all the while they slowly stretched their boughs to reach three hundred feet above the soil. A well-timed visit to Reflection Lakes and the subalpine region called Paradise will leave no doubt why that moniker applies. Some things, when you see them for the first time, create a stirring the heart can comprehend but the mind cannot explain. The encounter is unique to you, and despite how you may try, you can't adequately describe it to others.

Mystery and majesty surround *Tahoma*, as Mount Rainier was first called by the Salish Indians, who dwelt in its shadows and sought their daily sustenance in its forests, meadows, and rivers. They revered it for its perceived powers and for the dynamic ways it revealed wonder in beauty and bounty. The mountain gave them water to drink and food to eat. They believed there was something more to the mountain than what they could physically see; its magnificence and spectacle pointed to a presence greater than the capacity of their senses to know.

A rational person will concede that the mountain is still there, even when shrouded from sight by the clouds. A person of faith confesses that there is more to the mountain than meets the eye. The entire design of creation reveals the beauty of the creator (Psalm 19:1). This is the real allure of the mountain: it draws us toward that which is inscrutable and wholly Other, partially revealing through its splendor what is otherwise concealed.

The Orthodox church understood its icons as windows through which to encounter the Divine. Beauty such as Mount Rainier offers transient access to the great mysteries that are the wonder of creation—

and the subtle likeness of the One who created it. It is something we cannot view directly, lest it consume us, but we can catch a glimpse and we can wonder.

Spotted Owl

And if you get to Reflection Lake, be certain to stand in such a way that you see not only the mountain's reflection shimmering on the surface of the water, but your own as well.

Think about a time the Divine was revealed to you in nature. What made that experience different? How did it change or affect you? In what ways do you believe that you reflect the glory of God?

Deer at Paradise

NORTH CASCADES NATIONAL PARK

WASHINGTON • 1968 • PLACE

The high mountains are for the wild goats;
the rocks are a refuge for the rock badgers.
—PSALM 104:18 (ESV)

We need a space where we belong, one suited to our most basic needs and deepest desires. The creation poem in Genesis I, which Psalm 104 reflects upon, purposefully, but somewhat playfully, proclaims things are in their right place. The ordering of the world is not only a creative act, but it is about establishing what is normal and therefore what is "clean" or pure. This is so all things can flourish and achieve their best creative potential. The winged things that wing in the sky, the swimming things that swim in the sea, and the creeping things that creep on the land *belong* there.

When you read the names of the mountains in rugged, nearly road-less North Cascades National Park, you sense that the people who sought to settle the region felt they didn't belong in the harsh Cascade environment: Damnation Peak, Mt. Terror, Mt. Despair, Forbidden Peak, along with Devil's Pass and Three Fools' Creek! If you make the effort to venture here, you may find your place in some of the best mountain trails in the country. Your place in this land, where glaciers are melting at an alarming rate, may be to join the work to protect it before their place is forever lost to a changing climate.

When have you felt "out of place"? What does it mean to be in the right place? How does your faith help you come to know the place where you belong?

A solitary campsite with a view of Buckner Mountain and Boston Glacier

Sol Duc Falls

OLYMPIC NATIONAL PARK

WASHINGTON • 1938 • GIFTS

By the word of the LORD the heavens were made,
and all their host by the breath of his mouth.
He gathered the waters of the sea as in a bottle;
he put the deeps in storehouses.
Let all the earth fear the LORD;
let all the inhabitants of the world stand in awe of him.
For he spoke, and it came to be;
he commanded, and it stood firm.

—PSALM 33:6–9 (NRSV)

The largest concentration of life found on the planet is in the temperate rain forests of northwest Washington. The moss covers so much of the forest floor you may begin to think that if you pause anywhere too long it might just envelop you as well! There are trees that have been standing here since before Galileo peered at the heavens through his telescope, trees with a girth of up to 40 feet that reach 250 feet up into the sky. Salmon from the Pacific ascend waterfalls like staircases to move upstream, swimming toward their birthplace to reproduce the cycle that spawned them. Glacial snowmelt feeds arctic-cold and clear blue streams that quench the thirst of Roosevelt elk meandering below Mount Olympus's rocky shoulders.

The park includes miles of Pacific coastline and beyond the shoreline lies a silent testimony to the power of the ocean, which has left behind broken remnants of cliffs that once tried to constrain its tides. Along these beaches, the Pacific spits out driftwood composed of entire tree trunks, as if they were the spent toothpicks of some mythical giant. The churning waters are a marine sanctuary. Above the banks in mountain meadows, wildflowers toss in the winds, while Olympic marmots

Freshwater streams
permeate the park.

Split Rock at Rialto
Beach

chew on lupine leaves and glacier lilies. The marmots and elk you see here are native to this patch of ground and cannot be found anywhere else on earth.

Within the park boundaries, you can see the world's largest western hemlock, the nation's largest subalpine fir, giant Alaska cedars, enormous stands of Douglas fir, and rhododendrons thirty feet high. The sky is filled with bald eagles, osprey, and kingfishers angling for dinner. Coastal waters bounce tufted puffins along waves where sea lions and seals swim among starfish and oysters.

The Olympic Peninsula teems with so much life that the United Nations Education Scientific and Culture Organization has given the area biosphere reserve status in an effort to further protect the unique plant and animal life within its borders. To walk the Hoh River Trail is to contemplate Eden itself. What was it like when the world was young and undisturbed by the human quest to build, develop, and reshape all that we see? Filling your lungs at Sol Duc Falls carries the distant cosmic memory of the sweet first breath that gave life to our primordial ancestors.

This incredible diversity is created by the Olympic Mountain Range, which showers 150 inches of rainfall into the western portion of the park. Only 25 percent of that amount falls to the east, providing ambitious visitors very different varieties of life to discover if they take in both the leeward and windward sides of the slopes. It gives credit to the playful imagination of a Divine Creator and testifies to the wonders of evolutionary progress. Take your pick: either can inspire one who appreciates the complexity spread out before them.

Astute observers will quickly become aware of how fragile is the web that knits all of this life together. None of this is capable of existing without the other seemingly unrelated and distant parts of the whole. There are life lessons taught in the created order that we would do well to learn. There is a high concentration here of exceedingly diverse life living interdependently, resulting in unrivaled beauty. It is abundance and sufficiency that allows this environment to flourish, a delicate balance that should not be confused as excess. Nothing is wasted, as even that which falls to the forest floor in time becomes the renewing energy for growth to be sustained.

To see all of this is to come face-to-face with the knowledge that life itself is a gift and that your own life is connected in some marvelous and mysterious way to all other life on earth. The beauty and the wonder of our world may be something we can elect to manage or choose to exploit, but it is not something we can create.

When have you thought about your life as a gift? In what ways might you express gratitude for this gift? How might viewing the natural world as a gift change the way we steward these resources?

Hurricane Ridge looking toward the Olympic mountain range

PETRIFIED FOREST
NATIONAL PARK

ARIZONA • 1962 • TIME

For everything there is a season, and a time for every matter under heaven. . . .
[God] has made everything suitable for its time;
moreover he has put a sense of past and future into their minds. . . .
I know that whatever God does endures forever; nothing can be added to it,
nor anything taken from it; God has done this,
so that all should stand in awe before him.

—ECCLESIASTES 3:1, 11, 14 (NRSV)

Time is a way to talk about the constant progress of existence from the past, to the present, and on into the future. The Abrahamic religions brought the philosophical concept of linear time into human consciousness. In other religious traditions, time is cyclical, repeating itself in a never-ending spiral. But with sacred writings that put a starting and ending point on finite creation, time moves in one direction: forward.

Time also leaves a trail of where it has been. We call it history. Humans have left written and oral chronicles of the past. But the earth has recorded its own history without human aid by leaving traces of the past for us to discover. Petrified Forest National Park embodies this latter concept.

The main attraction is the mineral-filled wood. It is stunning to behold: bright ochre, red, orange, mustard, blue, purple, brown, white, and black. Each log is different, and its color depends on which trace elements the wood absorbed along with the silica that bonded with the cells and replicated them into quartz. These trees once lined an ancient riverbed. But if you go looking for a forest in the traditional sense, you will be disappointed at the moonscape that greets you. There are no

The Painted Desert can be seen from the northern end of the park.

Broken fossilized logs look as though they have been cut by a saw.

lush verdant valleys here. Those are a distant memory of a time when scientists believe that what is now the Colorado Plateau was once near the equator. The shifting landmasses pushed north what is now the North American continent.

The process to petrify wood and then reveal the wonder through erosion took over two hundred million years. Fascinating as the stone trees are lying in neatly segmented pieces on the desert floor as if sawn by a great lumberjack, there is more to the Petrified Forest than the wood! An immense geological record of the Triassic Period lies beneath the exposed logs. The fossilized remains of the early dinosaurs, those creatures that preceded the fabled Jurassic Period, are abundant, including crocodile-like reptiles over twenty-five feet in length that stalked this swamp with their razor-sharp teeth.

Time has also left a trail of human activity at the park. Ancient Puebloan remains and well-preserved petroglyphs mean that archeologists as well as paleontologists have an interest here. The indigenous people had their own interest in time, evidenced by a spiral rock carving that appears to have functioned as a solar calendar, marking the point of the summer solstice. Even the remnants of the early twenti-eth century have left a clear link to the past: the telegraph poles that lined the historic Route 66 testify to its having traversed the park's current boundaries. A 1932 Studebaker marks the spot where Ameri-ca's first interstate highway intersects the twenty-eight-mile road that bisects the park.

Time is a connecting fiber in our own web of meaning and under-standing. It is a shared element throughout the created order. It reminds us of where we have been. It locates us in the present and allows us to imagine ourselves in the future. It factors into the powerful gift of memory and participates in the marking of transformation and change. Time also reminds us that we are finite creatures and that while time is endless, we will enjoy only a limited supply of it. Eventually time will mark where our lives began and where they ended. This is why time is so precious and why what we do with it matters.

As you review how you use time, is there some time that you could put to better use? If you could spend more time doing something, what would it be, and with whom would you spend it? What is the legacy you want time to record about your life?

Rich colors from trace elements that bonded in the quartz

Pinnacles' high peaks at sunset

PINNACLES NATIONAL PARK

CALIFORNIA • 2013 • RETURN

And the ransomed of the LORD shall return,
and come to Zion with singing,
everlasting joy shall be upon their heads;
they shall obtain joy and gladness,
and sorrow and sighing shall flee away.

—ISAIAH 35:10 (NRSV)

"Which of these is not like the others?"—the game goes. At Pinnacles National Park, it's obvious that the rust-colored pinnacles from ancient volcanos look nothing like the surrounding hillsides. They simply don't match. Torn asunder from their original location and split by violent geological forces, these rugged peaks have ridden along the Pacific Plate, sliding two hundred miles northward along the San Andreas Fault, leaving their other "half" behind. They are a stunning and stark contrast to the gentle slopes and open valleys that sit below them. The peaks are still moving at a swift two inches per year, which by geological standards is Bonneville Salt Flats fast!

Over time wind, water, and plant life have formed steep canyons and fashioned huge boulders. As tectonic pressures build and release stress, the shaking earth causes these great stones to tumble into the canyons, creating talus caves. Streams in the canyons remove debris, clearing passageways through the caves and providing respite for animals escaping summer heat. High cliffs are home to nesting birds, while dense woody chaparral covers much of the lower countryside. Valley oak, gray pine, California buckeye, and other large trees add to the wide diversity of life that can be found here.

Hiking and climbing are popular in this park, as there is not much access by automobile. The High Peaks Trail is a testament to the efforts

Reintroduced through conservation, a California condor takes flight.

of the Civilian Conservation Corp, created during the Great Depression to give young men room, board, and meaningful labor along with a modest wage. Many national and state parks across the country benefited from their physical endeavors, and the buildings and trails they constructed in the 1930s remain. The rugged High Peaks Trail, with pathways and stairways carved out of solid rock and tunnels bored through the side of the mountains, rewards those who make the trek with panoramic views of the park and opportunities to see wildlife from a closer perspective.

The land here has been lived on, possessed by, or belonged to the Chalon and Mutsun tribes, Spanish missionaries, miners and prospectors, homesteaders, and the countries of Spain, Mexico, and eventually the United States. The land is now welcoming back one former resident that has been gone for eighty years: the California condor. This magnificent species was all but extinct by the 1980s, but careful conservation programs and intentional restoration projects are reintroducing the condor to the wild. Pinnacles is a release site for these massive scavengers who soar above the rocky peaks on 9 1/2-foot wingspans, seeking out carrion and keeping nature's life cycle balanced. The birds with their bald heads and gangly necks are not likely to win any beauty contests when at rest, but when they take to the sky and ride the rising thermals, they are awe-inspiring.

The condors' return to the skies is a triumph and a demonstration that we can reverse some of the damage we have done to our environment and the creatures who sprung from God's creative imagination. The condor is still endangered, but progress is being made as we return their world to a safer place for them that we can share. The sight of their return brings joy to us and perhaps to the Creator as well.

Return is an ongoing theme in the Bible. People are invited to return to the Lord, meaning making God their first love and priority. Prophets hold out return as an invitation not to escape punishment, but to respond to the gracious acts that God has already performed. It is the journey to find our true self that holds within it the image of the Divine in relationship and action. Prophets promise return for those in exile, an end to God's anger, and God's desire for reconciliation and restoration among people. The theme of return also pervades the New Testament—here specifically that of Jesus who will, at some point, set right all that is wrong and establish a peace that will be both final and eternal.

Bear Gulch Reservoir

To what place, time, or relationship would you like to return? What would you hope to gain by doing so? Does the idea of some kind of a return of God bring you hope?

REDWOOD NATIONAL AND
STATE PARKS

CALIFORNIA • 1968 • PEACE

Peace I leave with you; my peace I give to you. I do not give to you as the world
gives. Do not let your hearts be troubled, and do not let them be afraid.

—JOHN 14:27 (NRSV)

To walk among the redwood trees in the morning mist is to experience a peace that defies explanation. It is a place for quiet discernment about the directions of a life. One feels awe and wonder, not just in looking up at some of the tallest living things on earth, but in gazing across the landscape. One feels the tranquility in the streams trickling through moss-lined banks amid the ferns and understory growth, all dotted with the spotty shafts of light peeking through the canopy.

Despite beautiful prairies where grazing elk wander and rocky ocean beaches sprinkled with tide pools teeming with life, the redwood trees are the main attraction in this park. And why not? For at 350 feet they stand as powerful sentinels towering over the coastal grounds. Should Lady Liberty choose to leave the New York harbor, she could stand in the peaceful shade of these giants with room to spare.

It is ironic that a place where such serenity is found was born in struggle and controversy. When white Europeans first came to the coast ranges where the redwoods flourished, they bypassed the giant trees in favor of the smaller species that the logging equipment of the day could handle. The titanic trees were just too formidable for the ax alone to take down. In a relatively short time, however, advances in timber harvesting technology made the massive giants an obtainable and preferred target due to the high yield from a single tree. Unrelenting clear-cutting of the coast redwoods ran through much of the early twentieth century. By

Redwoods dwarf everything around them.

The Pacific coast frames the western edge of the park.

1929, five hundred million board feet were being harvested annually. As bulldozers, chainsaws, and trucks grew in size, so did the number of trees being cut to the ground.

Conservation efforts began in 1918, and eventually three California state parks were created to protect the magnificent trees. As more trees disappeared from the landscape, conservation efforts grew for their protection—but so did the defense of the logging industry's clear-cutting practice. It was a contentious battle with powerful economic interests on one side and university professors and ecologists on the other.

People who sought to place themselves between the redwoods and the lumber mills became known as "tree huggers"—not a complimentary term! Mounting pressure in favor of preservation from celebrities, politicians, and even the then First Lady of the United States, Lady Bird Johnson, eventually won the day, and Redwood National Park was born, sharing management of the existing lands of the state parks and preserves. When you consider that only 5 percent of the original old-growth forest remains, it is clear that such management did not happen a moment too soon.

The sound of the acorn woodpecker searching for a meal has replaced the sound of the ax, and the bugle of a male elk claiming this part of the woods as his territory, has replaced the rumble of the logging truck. It is hard to imagine what the world would be like if these tall trees had totally disappeared and what threat that would have meant to many already endangered species that call this forest home.

And there are scars. A close examination reveals efforts of restoration where lasting damage was done. The land bears the wounds where old-growth trees once stood and where new seedlings, carefully managed, are taking hold. The peace was hard won, which makes its sounds and its quiet that much sweeter and reverent.

Sometimes peace does not come without a struggle. According to the gospels, when Jesus offered his disciples lasting peace, it came only after a confrontation with death itself. Having been to hell and back, he bore the disfigurements of an ultimate conflict in which he prevailed and thereby won an essential and accessible peace for all.

What are the previously broken places in the landscape of your own life where you now find a sense of peace? When have you been unexpectedly "overwhelmed" by peace? Do you know someone anxious whom you might help find peace?

Fog in an ancient redwood grove

Two Rivers Lake, late May

ROCKY MOUNTAIN NATIONAL PARK

COLORADO • 1915 • PERSPECTIVE

I lift up my eyes to the mountains—
where does my help come from?
My help comes from the LORD,
the Maker of heaven and earth.

— PSALM 121:1–2 (NIV)

If you've had enough birthdays, you can't begin the drive along the forty-eight-mile Trail Ridge Road that traverses the park without imagining John Denver singing "Rocky Mountain High." The 1972 pop hit was inspired by a concern that real-estate development in the mountains would ruin the natural wonder that encompasses the barren, tundra-touched rock peaks and glacial valleys with woodlands, meadows, and meandering streams cascading down the mountainside through stands of golden aspen trees.

Nature's sounds in the Rocky Mountain National Park are enchanting. A visit in the right season brings the distinctive bugle of bull elks calling their harems as they claim grazing territory, the echoing crack of bighorn sheep rams battling to establish dominance for mating, and the songs of any of the three hundred species of birds that can be found there. Add the sound of the wind speaking its presence in the branches of Great Basin bristlecone pines or subalpine firs that reach to touch the sky; water rushing over rock as it seeks the sea; and the symphony of a thousand quiet noises made by all of the living things that surround you and you know that there is something special about the place in which you stand.

Mountains have a sense of the sacred about them. The faith traditions of Moses, Jesus, and Muhammad each have stories of Divine

U.S. Geological Survey marker atop Longs Peak

encounters related to specific high places, fixed points of geography to mark mystical experiences that defy temporal definition. Mountains are places of radical change, new perspective, and heightened awareness. There is such a universal acceptance of this concept that *the mountaintop* is synonymous with a life-altering experience in how we see this world or the next. Consider Martin Luther King Jr.'s reference to having "been to the mountaintop," from his speech in Memphis the night before he was assassinated. Mountains are the places for visions and reality checks, for reflection and possibility.

The journey up the mountain can be perilous. Even if trading carabiners and crampons for the family sedan, you have to be careful in the climb. Intent focus on where you are and what is immediately around you is essential for a successful ascent. (If you are hiking, drink plenty of water to help control altitude sickness.) Upon reaching the summit, however, details of the close-at-hand are exchanged for the distant horizon. The energy expended to reach the top is traded for deep breaths of exhilaration in what is revealed when nothing remains to obstruct your view. From here, you can see where you have been and where you might go next. This perspective allows you to see how things fit together, to identify why parts of the road traveled were difficult or easy. The world is a beautiful and awesome place full of terrors and wonders alike. Yet despite your apparent insignificance against such a grand and sweeping scale, you are a part of it all.

Such a perspective is a method of reorienting life around the Why? and What matters most? sometimes begging the essential questions Who am I? and What am I supposed to do? Mystics refer to these moments and places as the *thin spaces* where we can draw closer to that which is greater than ourselves.

Rocky Mountain National Park offers plenty of things to amaze, but whatever inspires you will be meaningless without application, which is always done down the mountain. Even the snow that falls in these heights will descend as water for life below. Some of the waters will be gathered as the Colorado River, and seven southwestern states and parts of Mexico will benefit from its transformation as it pours itself out in the Gulf of California. Some of the water will gather into the Platte, Missouri, and Mississippi Rivers, watering another eleven states.

What has been a recent "mountaintop" experience in your life? How have you taken that experience "down the mountain" and applied it to your daily living? What in your life could benefit from a change in perspective?

Bighorn rams on the tundra

SAGUARO NATIONAL PARK

ARIZONA • 1994 • NURTURE

The LORD is your keeper;
the LORD is your shade at your right hand.
The sun shall not strike you by day, nor the moon by night.
The LORD will keep you from all evil;
he will keep your life.

—PSALM 121:5–7 (NRSV)

Saguaro cacti are the most recognized symbol of the American West. When we see these almost human-looking cacti with their stalwart arms, we know we are in the desert. Encountered in person, saguaro (Sa-WHAR-o) are magnificent and imposing. Growing over fifty feet tall, weighing up to eight tons, with a girth of over ten feet, and covered in scalpel-sharp needles, they are a testament to resilience, adaptation, and ecological interdependence. They store vast quantities of water—over 1,500 gallons from a single rainstorm. They produce upward of forty million seeds in a 150-year lifespan, and humans and desert wildlife alike prize their fruit. Saguaro provide shelter, food, and protection.

Yet despite their imposing nature, saguaro are fragile. A freeze lasting more than a few hours will kill even the biggest cacti. Despite the incredible number of seeds they produce, only a scant few (perhaps only one) will survive, and ten years may see only two inches of growth in the seed fortunate enough to take root! The first of its distinctive arms appear only after fifty years of growth. A giant saguaro's best chance of survival comes if it is fortunate enough to grow in the shadow of a "nurse tree," usually ironwood or palo verde shrubs, which provide shade from the desert sun and protection from being uprooted by a passing gray fox or javelina.

A giant saguaro

The desert blooms even in the heat of summer.

As the saguaro grows, it will serve for decades as a life-giving station in the midst of desert barrenness. Woodpeckers will bore holes in its trunk searching for insects and moisture. Those holes then become nests for cactus wrens to raise their young. Kestrels (small hawks) gather debris from the desert floor to build their own nests in the space between the arms and the trunk of the plant. The late spring blooms of its beautiful white flowers, the Arizona state flower, give nectar to migrating hummingbirds and attract insects, which will in turn feed birds in the daylight and bats by moonlight. Lizards and reptiles gather food and water from the saguaro while using its needles as a defense against other predators. When early summer ripens the fruit, it feeds a host of desert wildlife and even finds its way onto human tables as a jam or sauce. Its shallow root system, which spreads away from the plant in a distance equal to the saguaro's height, gathers even small amounts of rainwater with incredible efficiency and helps prevent erosion of the desert soil.

Magnificent as it is, with so many creatures depending on its life for their own, it also depends on something else for its survival—the nurse tree that it will eventually both outgrow and outlive. Nothing survives alone in the desert, no matter how big or small.

We, like the saguaro, depend on nurture to survive. For the human community to thrive, we must receive and be willing to give nurture. It is not simply the image of the tender care a mother gives to a vulnerable infant, but rather a strong sense of advocacy for our fellow sojourners on this planet that can enrich our lives and secure our future. Our humanity carries with it a charge from God that we might exercise our humanity in a way similar to the way God cares for the cosmos: seeking its ultimate benefit so that it can realize its best positive potential.

In the Gospel of Matthew, Jesus says that in order for us to see the realm of God we must feed the hungry, give water to the thirsty, clothe the naked, care for the sick, and visit the prisoner. Sounds a lot like nurture! Perhaps you'll look at the ironwood and palo verde beside the giant saguaro in a new way with such nurture in mind.

From whom have you received nurture in your life? How has that nurture affected your life and made you who you are? Who do you know who could benefit from some nurture from you?

Nurse tree with multiple saguaros

SEQUOIA NATIONAL PARK

CALIFORNIA • 1890 • FOUNDATION

"Everyone who hears these words of mine and puts them into practice is like a wise man who built his house on the rock."

—MATTHEW 7:24 (NIV)

They're almost too big to believe. Giant sequoia trees are tall, but there are taller trees elsewhere in California. It's the circumference, the depth, the sheer volume of life in front of you embodied in one of the planet's largest organisms that is jaw-dropping.

When you drive into Sequoia National Park heading for the main attractions, you set your eyes on the granite peak of Moro Rock, more than a thousand feet of sheer cliffs towering over the Kaweah River. Then you follow one of the curviest roads you'll ever enjoy to scale the side of Moro Rock and the appropriately named Switchback Mountain. Eventually the road straightens out, and you enter the Giant Forest. Interspersed among the pines are immense cinnamon-hued trunks that are branchless for dozens of feet till they begin, dizzyingly high. When you can see the top of the column-like tree, often it's not the pointed top you expect from mountain trees. Lightning frequently prunes the tops of the sequoias, leaving them blunt and a bit charred. The further you drive and the higher your altitude, the more of these trees you see. These are the great sequoias, with the fantastically appropriate scientific name *Sequoiadendron giganteum*.

A short hike takes you to General Sherman, the world's largest known tree. Not the tallest, nor the widest, nor the oldest, but don't let the lack of superlatives lower your expectations. General Sherman is the largest by volume and by weight. A sign at the tree's base states it could hold enough water to fill almost ten thousand bathtubs, and that it weighs about 1,385 tons. Estimated at 2,200 years old—let that soak

Giant Forest

in—the tree is more than 36 feet across at the base and towers 274 feet above you, which gives us the unique perspective of a flea gazing up at a gigantic human.

In the era of logging and churning through natural resources, timber companies imagined how much money they could make harvesting sequoias. But the trees foiled their plans by being brittle; trees shattered when they crashed to the ground. Brittle wood was of little practical use, and logging ended in the 1920s.

Brittle, though, doesn't mean weak. Giant sequoias are surprisingly resistant to fire, and they actually need fire to continue as a species. Walk through a grove, and you'll see giant sequoias thoroughly scorched, sometimes with large hollows in the trunk at ground level. But those trees continue to thrive, thanks in part to bark up to thirty inches

Moro Rock and the Kaweah River

thick. Fire triggers the opening of giant sequoia cones and thins out the ecosystem, giving seeds a better chance at germination and survival. Controlled burns and closely monitored wildfires are tolerated in the interest of future trees.

Sequoias thrive only in a few places; there are fewer than seventy known groves, and in the United States they are concentrated in the Sierra Nevada near Sequoia and adjacent Kings Canyon National Parks. Usually found in humid climates with snowy winters and dry summers, giant sequoias stick to the higher elevations between five and seven thousand feet. In the dry air, the trees have a sophisticated system to push water absorbed by the roots up the trunk and to use air roots to absorb moisture from fog.

It's easy to believe these immense trees were made especially for this rare place on earth: high above the ocean, just the right amount of rock in the soil, with the right kind of moisture in the right places. If you happen upon a toppled tree and see its root ball, ridiculously big, you may start imagining around you the deep roots necessary to hold such a large structure upright. Those roots have dug deep for a long, long time—much longer than you've been alive.

No matter how mighty the tree, it would collapse and die without the roots as its foundation. We thinking humans have different kinds of foundations: Our moral codes that help us make decisions every day, whether we realize our morals are at play or not. We turn off the water while brushing our teeth so we don't waste water. We recycle. We turn off our car engine while waiting to pick up our kids after school even if it's hot or cold. We vote our consciences. Our foundation is there, keeping our souls steady. We know when we stray from that foundation because we become disoriented, unsteady, unsure. We topple, even if it's just for a moment.

What have been your life's foundations? Could your foundation use some shoring up? How can you serve as a foundation for somebody important to you?

Skyline Drive in autumn

SHENANDOAH NATIONAL PARK

Look down from your holy house in Heaven! Bless your people Israel and the
ground you gave us, just as you promised our ancestors you would,
this land flowing with milk and honey.

—DEUTERONOMY 26:15 (MESSAGE)

For millions of Americans, Shenandoah National Park is their neighborhood national park. Just seventy-five miles from the nation's capital and a few hundred miles from the East Coast megalopolis stretching from D.C. north to New York City, Shenandoah was created partly in response to the majority of early national parks being located out west. Two parks—Maine's Acadia and Great Smoky Mountains spanning the Tennessee-North Carolina border—partially filled that void, but the long ridgeline through north-central Virginia became a project for Virginia leaders in the years leading up to the Great Depression.

The challenge was that the land had been occupied for generations by subsistence farmers and tradesmen living in small communities or in their own isolation. Despite their hard way of life and an exhausted landscape, convincing them to leave their homes was not an easy task.

Cobbling together the park wasn't easy either. The original vision for the park required obtaining more than five thousand parcels of land, and the federal government provided no funding for the park. Virginia political and civic leaders raised money to buy the land, scraped together some public money, and changed laws to make it easier for them to acquire the land. But many residents, especially older ones who had always lived in the Shenandoah highlands, refused to sell at any price.

Thinking creatively, park supporters crafted a compromise: residents could remain on their land the rest of their lives. Steadfast residents agreed, and eventually the federal government accepted the deal. The last grandfathered resident, Annie Lee Bradley Shenk, passed away in 1979, more than three decades after her husband preceded her.

The Great Depression, a tree blight, and the opportunity to improve their quality of life prompted most of the more than two thousand residents to leave their homes in the early years. Much of the evidence of those old homesteads has been removed, but a few hollows still hold cemeteries and other artifacts of the people who used to call Shenandoah home.

The park was transformed by the construction of Skyline Drive, a twisting 105-mile, two-lane road. For many visitors, what they see from Skyline Drive is all they will ever see of the park. And that's just fine, for dozens of pullouts provide vast views of the Shenandoah River valley to the west and the Piedmont to the east. No view is the same, and you could spend your whole trip gazing out at your favorite vista. As you make your way along the road, keep your eyes open for a black bear traipsing along the side of the road, deer skittering into the woods, or foxes and bobcats. The speed limit along Skyline Road is thirty-five miles per hour, which may feel too fast as you take in the views from mountains billions of years old.

Shenandoah's rolling hills

But to examine those mountains up close or to see the old backcountry homes, you will need to get out of your car and hike. With more than five hundred miles of trails of varying difficulty, there is a trail for every ability. The Appalachian

Trail, stretching from Georgia to Maine, passes through the park and crisscrosses many of the smaller trails along the way. Limberlost Trail is accessible to all and showcases the flora of Virginia, especially mountain laurel in June. Another popular trail takes you through a valley shaded by oak, maple, hickory, and other trees and leads to Dark Hollow Falls, which stairsteps seventy feet under a lush canopy. Blackrock Summit Trail connects to a rock jumble that will entertain rock scramblers for hours. Other trails will take you to the park's high points at Hawksbill Mountain (elevation 4,051 feet), Stony Man (4,011 feet), and Old Rag (3,291).

Once the day is done, you can relax at developed or backcountry campgrounds or huts along the Appalachian Trail. If you want something a little more luxurious, Skyland has offered accommodations since the 1890s; its owner was one of the visionaries for the park, seeing the economic opportunities in potential tourists. You can also visit the mountain retreat of former President Herbert Hoover, who donated his Rapidan Camp to the park when he left office.

Eventually, you will head back home, but perhaps you will understand why so many old-timers didn't want to leave the beautiful mountains their families had called home for generations. Maybe Shenandoah will become a home away from home for you too.

Where are the places you have called home? What is it about those places that have truly made them feel like home? How you can help others make a new place their home?

THEODORE ROOSEVELT NATIONAL PARK

NORTH DAKOTA · 1978 · VISION

At once the Spirit sent him out into the wilderness, and he was in the wilderness
forty days. . . . He was with the wild animals, and angels attended him.
After John was put in prison, Jesus went into Galilee, proclaiming the good news
of God. "The time has come," he said. "The kingdom of God has come near.
Repent and believe the good news!"

—MARK 1:12–15 (NIV)

On a dark September night in 1883, a scrawny, bespectacled twenty-five year-old from New York City stepped off a train at the western edge of the Dakota Territory. Theodore Roosevelt had come west to hunt bison. While his pregnant wife, Alice, waited back home, Teddy fell in love with the western skies, the rolling Badlands, and the cowboy lifestyle of the northern frontier. Before his two-week vacation ended, he purchased a ranch, probably expecting to return soon with his family for more adventures in the Wild West.

Less than a year later, Roosevelt returned a broken man. In the span of three days, he became a father, lost his mother—then, horrifyingly, his wife. Grieving and seeking solace, Roosevelt fled back to Dakota that summer. It may be hard to imagine now, but Roosevelt may have teetered on the edge of choosing ranching over politics.

While in Dakota, Roosevelt discovered that "the West" was already disappearing. The bison that once rumbled in uncountable numbers were now scarce herds, thinned by settlers and railroads. Cattle overgrazed the land, and other wildlife like elk and bighorn sheep were rare. Tellingly, he arrived as the displacement of Native Americans—the people who for generations stewarded the land that sustained them—wound down. Truth be told, Roosevelt saw the results of westward

Prairie sunset

expansion, and recognized what had already been destroyed. The lesson stuck with him.

During his stays at the Elkhorn Ranch, he wrote and relaxed and ranched and hunted and joined in roundups—and found clarity about his next steps in life. Roosevelt advised presidential candidates, lost the New York City mayoral race, remarried, became a father several more times, and published several books. In 1898, while serving as assistant secretary of the Navy, the Spanish-American War broke out. Roosevelt resigned the administrative post to lead the "Rough Riders," the legendary brigade that found glory in Cuba. By the end of the year, Roosevelt had been elected governor of New York. His national profile soared. Two years later, he was vice president.

Then came the shocking assassination of President William McKinley. At forty-two, Roosevelt, the man who only a few years earlier was as likely a cattle rancher in the North Dakota plains as a war hero and international leader, became the president of the United States.

Roosevelt is remembered for many things, but he is widely admired as the conservation president. His 1906 signing of the Antiquities Act preserved more than 230 million acres—an area larger than New Mexico, Arizona, and Nevada combined—creating more than two hundred federally protected areas, the basis of today's National Park Service and U.S. Forest Service.

"We have become great because of the lavish use of our resources," Roosevelt proclaimed to a national conference of governors in 1908. "But the time has come to inquire seriously what will happen when our forests are gone, when the coal, the iron, the oil, and the gas are exhausted, when the soils have still further impoverished and washed into the streams, polluting the rivers, denuding the fields and obstructing navigation."

His remarkable political success or his war-hero status could have erased those formative Dakota days, but he never forgot them. "I have always said," Roosevelt proclaimed, "I would not have been President had it not been for my experience in North Dakota." Roosevelt's love for the prairies is memorialized in this national park, the only one named for a president.

The park's history begins sixty-five million years ago, just after the dinosaur extinction, when the Rockies were new, volcanoes spewed ash, and the prairies were covered with layer upon layer of sediment. Then wind and water and cold shaped the land, exposing the colorful layers and sculpting the rolling hills Roosevelt loved. "Nowhere, not even at sea, does a man feel more lonely than when riding over the far-reaching, seemingly never-ending plains; and after a man has lived a little while on or near them, their very vastness and loneliness and their melancholy monotony have a strong fascination for him." Those same plains, Roosevelt's cabin, and restored bison, elk, deer, feral horses, prairie dogs, porcupines, beavers, coyotes, can still inspire you today.

Roosevelt's vision of preserving America's natural wonders traces its roots back to this place. What are the places that inspire you? What changes do you want to see—in yourself, in your faith, in your world? How can you live into the change God calls you to make?

An elk harem

Salomon Beach

VIRGIN ISLANDS
NATIONAL PARK

U.S. VIRGIN ISLANDS • 1956 • REMEMBER

Then they remembered his words.

—LUKE 24:8 (NRSV)

The sign at the entry to Virgin Islands National Park says, "Welcome to Paradise." To gaze on the white sand and the clear blue water, to hear exotic birds calling, and to see it all framed with palm and mangrove trees caressed by gentle trade winds is to know that the sign tells the truth! For many visitors, a trip to the U.S. Virgin Islands is the vacation of a lifetime, a destination for both making and celebrating memories.

The beaches and ocean provide a place to sail the tranquil waters or to dive to see the coral reefs, watch the colorful fish, or just to splash among the waves. Three different species of sea turtles—the hawksbill, the green, and the leatherback—nest here. The only time these magnificent creatures return to land is to lay their eggs. The females will return twenty-five years later to this same stretch of shoreline to restart the cycle. Somehow, they remember from whence they came.

At Trunk Bay, you can take the Rivsnorkel Trail where you use fins instead of shoes to follow interpretive signs about what you are swimming past. Bird-watchers will appreciate more than 140 species of avian visitors and yearlong residents of the island. The park service provides a checklist so you can remember what you have spotted.

Inland you will find the historic record of early inhabitants in petroglyphs. The hilly terrain includes a tropical forest filled with birds, reptiles, and an unlimited variety of insects, scorpions, spiders, and millipedes. The park literature helps you get from *ewwwww* to awe about the

Yellow jack, found over outer reefs

bugs, once you realize their importance to the environment. Not only are they food for birds, bats, and reptiles, but they break down fallen vegetation and thus reduce the possibility of wildfires. Bats are the only mammals indigenous to St. John's; all the others were introduced by humans, and this has not always worked out as planned. One invasive species, the mongoose, has become a significant problem. Brought here to control rats, they preferred instead to feast on bird and turtle eggs. Someone did not remember that rats are nocturnal and mongoose are not!

There is archeological evidence that humans came to St. John's from South America about 2,500 years ago. Taino people from the Amazon basin arrived later, within the last thousand years. Columbus, in a failed attempt to find a passage to India, "discovered" the Virgin Islands in 1493; the colonial powers of the English, Spanish, French, and Dutch followed, along with the pirates and privateers. They brought a thirst for resources and established more than one hundred sugarcane plantations. They also transported enslaved West Africans to work the sugar mills. Preserved remains of the machinery for sugar production are historical sites in the park, a reminder of the economic and political history of this land and the cruel practice of enslaving other human beings. Slavery ended here in 1848, long before the United States purchased this territory in 1919. Can you taste the irony of this tropical wonderland and the freedom stolen from an entire race of people? It is important to remember.

The biblical witness uses the term *remember* or *remembered* 286 times in the New Revised Standard Version. Memory matters. Sometimes we would rather forget. In the Scriptures, people beg God to forget their misdeeds all the time! But Scripture also urges the people to remember: to remember what God has done, to remember to honor their covenant with God, to remember the poor and the widow and stranger. It reminds Israel to remember who they are in light of how God defines them as "God's people." It urges the early church to remember the teachings of Jesus and the apostles and thus to define itself by its own faithfulness to these truths.

Sometimes, to remember is to avoid repeating a mistake in the future. Other times it can jolt us awake with sadness or joy. Remembering can even create an "aha!" moment that can change us forever. In the act of Communion, Christians believe the act of remembering puts you in the very presence of Jesus.

What is your earliest memory? Has suddenly remembering something ever changed a decision you were about to make? Can you think of a common memory that defines you or a group to which you belong?

Cinnamon Bay factory remains

VOYAGEURS NATIONAL PARK

MINNESOTA • 1975 • TEAMWORK

[Jesus] called his disciples to him and chose twelve of them,
whom he also designated apostles.

—LUKE 6:13 (NIV)

American lore celebrates the individual—adventuring solo into the wilderness, surviving the dangers, and carving a living out of the God-given resources. Voyageurs National Park, on the American-Canadian border in far northern Minnesota, corrects that myth, and instead honors the teamwork and cooperation that made survival possible.

For a century, traders known as *voyageurs* plied these waters, trading with Native American and First Nation hunters to obtain the beaver pelts Europeans craved, then paddling hundreds of miles to the eastern seaports. A tough life required tough workers, and the French-Canadian voyageurs are legendary in Canadian history and culture. With the lakes frozen over during the bitter winters, long summer days were consumed with paddling—more than 45,000 strokes per day! Portaging ninety pounds of beaver pelts was a common chore. Being a voyageur could be mind-numbing, monotonous work . . . and dangerous too.

But instead of a lonely explorer, the voyageur was part of a team, a pack of siblings in the wilderness who sang, ate, and worked together. Today, the highlight of a visit to Voyageurs National Park might be getting out on the lakes in a twenty-six-foot-long North Canoe, joining with a dozen other visitors to recreate that gritty life. Paddling a boat that size alone would be difficult, if not impossible, but teaming up proves that working together makes the job easier and more rewarding.

Where in your life do you team up with others? How can you be a better team leader or teammate? In what contexts of your life do you need to build new teams?

Experience the voyageur life with your crewmates.

Inside the mapped
portion of Wind Cave

WIND CAVE NATIONAL PARK

SOUTH DAKOTA • 1903 • SPIRIT

The wind blows where it chooses, and you hear the sound of it,
but you do not know where it comes from or where it goes.
So it is with everyone who is born of the Spirit.

—JOHN 3:8 (NRSV)

Above ground, Wind Cave National Park is a mixed-grass prairie where bison, elk, deer, and antelope roam. Woodlands and prairie meet here, so it is common to hear the song of the western meadow lark and the black-capped chickadee at the same time. Badgers and prairie dogs can be seen on the same hike as red squirrels and chipmunks.

Bison are the largest land mammal in North America, and you will find them here. An estimated thirty million bison once inhabited the land in the early 1800s, an ecological force upon the land. Native Americans valued them for food, clothing, shelter, and tools. They had an unorthodox method of hunting bison: herding them toward a "buffalo jump" (a cliff) where in the fury of a stampede, the poorly sighted animals could not avoid the precipice and thus plunged to their death. Nothing from the kill was wasted.

The onslaught of white European expansion westward decimated the buffalo by the power of the gun, reducing the tens of millions to less than one thousand animals by 1880. Traders prized tongues and skins, but many animals were shot for sport or with the intent to drive Native Americans onto reservations by depriving them of their primary resource.

Bison conservation was established at Wind Cave in 1913, and it is the oldest of four Great Plains parks where government management of the buffalo takes place. They are considered both wildlife and a conservation project, which means that they are managed for genetic

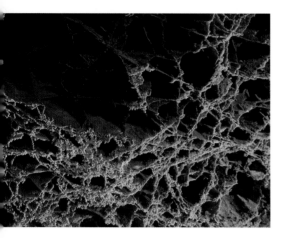

Rare cave formation boxwork

integrity, and that population density is controlled within park boundaries for the health of the herd while being left free of human interference as much as possible.

Below the bison range is one of the longest and most complex caves in the world—143 miles of known cave, fitting into just over one square mile. It possesses beautiful and rare geological formations like boxwork, found in few other places. A water source for eight states, the Madison aquifer flows in open pools hidden in the cave's depths.

And then there is the wind. Native people believe this to be a place of great spiritual power. Science says it is the changing barometric pressure that alternately pushes air in or out a small hole that is the original entrance to the cave. Lakota Tribes referred to the wind as Maka Oniye, *the earth is breathing*. The Sioux and Cheyenne cultures have a historic relationship to the cave and its mysterious breath. In these traditions, humans and the "four legged ones" emerged from the earth. Emergence stories are part of their creation stories of origin, and Wind Cave is where both humans and the buffalo found their way to the earth's surface. The buffalo is seen as a gift from the spirits to the native people. "Follow the buffalo track and you will have what you need" is a common refrain in the narrative, and for this reason native people consider both the animal and the cave as sacred.

Breath and wind have associations with the mysteries of the spirit world in most major religions. *Ru'ach* in Hebrew, *pneuma* in Greek, *spirit* in English: all seek to convey something that is sensed but unseen. To seek the spirit is to venture toward knowing something that cannot be fully known. The spirit can have creative power, the ability to reveal divine action or attributes, the power to influence human behavior, and it can disturb or alter the corporal world. It is transcendent and often mediates between the worlds of the finite and the infinite. The spirit is something to which humans respond, not something they can control. To be led by the spirit is understood in some traditions as to be lured by the sacred to seek the greater good, not only for oneself, but for others.

How or when have you experienced a sense of the presence of the Holy Spirit or its leading? Have you known people who seem to have a deep intimacy with the Divine by their encounter with the Spirit? Western faith expressions have often traded the value of intellectual knowledge over that gained by mystical encounters. What has been gained and lost in that exchange?

A buffalo jump

WRANGELL–ST. ELIAS NATIONAL PARK AND PRESERVE

ALASKA • 1980 • GUIDANCE

You're my cave to hide in, my cliff to climb.
Be my safe leader, be my true mountain guide.
Free me from hidden traps;
I want to hide in you.
I've put my life in your hands.
You won't drop me, you'll never let me down.

—Psalm 31:3–5 (Message)

Wrangell–St. Elias National Park and Preserve is the epitome of rugged. Nine of America's sixteen tallest mountains are found here including Mount St. Elias, America's second-tallest peak at 18,008 feet. America's largest national park could hold six Yellowstones. Malaspina Glacier alone could cover Rhode Island. Only McCarthy Road penetrates the center of the park, and its fifty-nine miles can take three hours to traverse, assuming your car survives the trip. If you want to go all the way to the town of McCarthy, you will drive to the end of the road, cross a footbridge, then take a shuttle.

The visiting season is generally a little more than four months, and winters are long and fierce. To explore Wrangell-St. Elias the wise tourist will connect with guides. Those guides will share their knowledge of the terrain, their wisdom, and the lessons the land can teach us. Being with those who have traveled the road before can spare us from hard lessons, or they can make those hard lessons easier to learn.

Admitting you don't know it all, that you'll need help, can be the first step toward change and understanding. Where do you need guidance in your life? Who can be your guide? How can you be a guide to others?

The Chitina River

Old Faithful erupts on an autumn afternoon.

YELLOWSTONE NATIONAL PARK

Praise GOD, everybody!
Applaud GOD, all people!
His love has taken over our lives;
GOD's faithful ways are eternal.
Hallelujah!

—PSALM 117:1–2 (MESSAGE)

Yellowstone. Images of the great American national park spring to mind: spewing geysers, soaring mountains, thundering water-falls, messy mud pots, raging rivers, tranquil buffalo, curious bears, petrified wood, skulking wolves, hard winters and glorious summers—the American wild. Yellowstone is the wildest of the parks, even if it is also one of the most visited parks.

Above all, it was the first. Native Americans told stories of a sacred place at the headwaters of the Yellowstone River. Explorers and trap-pers told incredulous stories of a place with sulfurous gasses, spewing water, and boiling mud. Eventually, Ulysses S. Grant signed legislation creating the world's first national park, tucked away in the Wyoming Territory.

In the years since, Yellowstone's reputation has spread around the world, attracting more than three million visitors annually. The languages spoken around the Grand Prismatic Pool evoke Babel, but the looks on the faces are united in amazement and delight at the natu-ral circus surrounding them.

What sets Yellowstone apart from the other parks are the unsur-passed geothermal miracles, and we have a still-brewing volcano to thank for them. With dimensions of roughly thirty by fifty miles, this volcano erupted most recently about 640,000 years ago, blasting a huge hole in the center of what is now Yellowstone. What we see now has had plenty of time to recover from what was, at the time, an unmitigated catastrophe. If that volcano were to erupt today, it would easily rank as the most devastating disaster in human history.

As that volcano simmers below the surface, water seeps in and boils, fueling Yellowstone's extravaganza. At the park's northern edge, Mammoth Hot Springs creates a terraced stairstep of steaming water, constantly changing and shifting. The Fountain Paint Pot slurps and burps gas from the bowels of the earth. At the Grand Prismatic Spring, 370 feet across, from the right angle one can see what appears to be a rainbow under the water but is actually different species of algae and bacteria that thrive in different temperatures of water ranging up to 160 degrees Fahrenheit. Nearby opal blue Excelsior Springs gushes four thousand gallons of scalding water into the Firehole River every minute. Driving through the park, there are so many steaming pools along the road that they become almost commonplace.

Geysers, though, are the main attraction, in part because of their unpredictability. Superheated water rockets through the underground tubes, jetting out in plumes that can reach three hundred feet in height. Each eruption is different, which is the blessing and the curse. Most of the geysers don't work on regular schedules; they erupt when they're ready, whether that's every few hours or every few decades. So don't plan to wait for lunch till that random geyser erupts. You may get very hungry.

Yet there is one exception to that general rule: Old Faithful. Perhaps the world's most famous geothermal feature, this geyser erupts with surprising regularity, roughly every ninety minutes, give or take, depending on how intense the previous eruption was. Any time of year, any kind of weather, odds are somebody is near Old Faithful, listening for the hollow gurgle that spits up water for a few minutes as a teaser for the main show. On windy days, a plume of mist blows into the crowd a taste of nature's greatest performance.

Yellowstone has its oddities, but it is also home to the densest animal population in the Lower 48. A huge wildlife preserve, Yellowstone offers opportunities to see the classic American animals of the West—namely bison and bears, both grizzly and black—from the safety of your car, as rangers remind you. There's no guarantee you'll see them,

Grand Prismatic Spring

but keep your eyes peeled and you may be rewarded.

Yellowstone was created in part to keep one of the world's most awe-inspiring places pristine, to demonstrate our faithfulness to protect God's creation. How we demonstrate that faithfulness creates controversy, from allowing wildfires to burn extensively while restoring the landscape or reintroducing wolves after they had been eradicated from the park. Passions run high over this special place, a testament to how much we adore it.

In our lives, we strive to be faithful: to keep our word to God and to each other, to treat each other like the holy creations we are, to see God in every living thing.

When have you most felt your faith at work? Where do you see growing edges in your faith? How can you help others strengthen their faith in God and in each other?

YOSEMITE NATIONAL PARK

CALIFORNIA · 1890 · TRUST

Trust in the LORD forever,
for in the LORD GOD
you have an everlasting rock.
—ISAIAH 26:4 (NRSV)

To see the Yosemite Valley in the "golden hour" prior to sunset from Tunnel View is to experience one of the most sublime vistas in the world. If there is a place that can stir the human conscience to search for traces of the Divine present in temporal space, it is at the Tunnel View overlook. There you see a verdant valley—carpeted with California black oak, ponderosa pine, incense cedar, and white fir—which the Merced River carved out of pure granite. The El Capitan monolith rises 3,500 feet from the valley floor, reflecting back the orange, red, and purple hues of waning sunlight. Half Dome rises 4,700 feet above the valley, its smooth and partially rounded surface mirroring the sun like a giant lighthouse. A misty thread of water, teased by the gentle wind, escapes a narrow cleft in the rock and catches fragments of golden light as it tumbles more than six hundred feet from Summit Meadow and creates Bridalveil Fall. As the setting sun floods the valley with its warm light, one simply runs out of adjectives to capture in words or thought the unfolding splendor.

Yosemite is fields of wildflowers, spectacular waterfalls, clear rivers and deep lakes, Jeffrey pines (whose bark smells like vanilla!), wetlands, mountains, and miles of hiking trails that climb thousands of feet of elevation in a breathtakingly short amount of distance but that reward you with views that will blow your mind with creation's beauty. Groves of sequoia trees, among the tallest living things on earth, dot the western and southern edges of Yosemite's boundaries. History records

Yosemite Falls

Merced River in winter

that John Muir and Theodore Roosevelt camped for several days in Yosemite, an experience that inspired the president to establish five national parks plus twenty-three national monuments and 150 national forests, marking them for protection and preserving them as a legacy in trust to the future generations.

Seeing photographs and reading about experiences through others are enough to recognize the importance of the heritage of the National Park System. But to go and see it for yourself is not only to appreciate the wisdom of those who have saved these sacred spaces, but to be overwhelmed with gratitude that they have done so. They have passed on to us a mantle of trust to preserve this wonder for those who come after us. We can imagine people yet to be born trusting us to do the same.

Trust is on full display in Yosemite at El Capitan. Daily, dozens of helmeted climbers put their trust in ropes, cams, carabiners, and quickdraws as they make an assault on the rock wall that has over two dozen established routes or "traditional climbs" with names like The Salathe Wall, Moby Dick, Peter Pan, Little John, Zodiac, Short but Thin, and the Nose. Different routes come with different challenges and test the climber's skill set. Ascents can take many days, so it is common to see climbers at varying altitudes sleeping in "slings," trusting their protection equipment to work and hold them fast to rock. After watching the daring hug sheer granite wall and grasp for a tight grip or a place with sure footing, it's no surprise to learn that the world-recognized scale to rate the difficulty of a rock climb is called the Yosemite Scale.

If the earth itself is any reflection of the work of a Divine creative imagination, and the glory and splendor we witness are but a faint echo of such craftsmanship, then such a being would not only be worthy of our praise but also of our trust based on ability and strength alone. Add to that the sacred narratives that speak to the

Climbing gear

faithfulness of the Holy One and God's nature as an advocate for and lover of creation, and confidence in God seems well placed and solid as a rock.

Whom or what do you trust and why? How does having trust in someone make it easier to take a risk in relationships or activities? Are you a person whom others might list as someone they trust?

Yosemite valley from Tunnel View

The Narrows

ZION NATIONAL PARK

Great is the LORD and greatly to be praised
in the city of our God.
His holy mountain, beautiful in elevation,
is the joy of all the earth,
Mount Zion, in the far north,
the city of the great King.
Within its citadels God
has shown himself a sure defense.

—PSALM 48:1–3 (NRSV)

When do you feel closer to God: in a sanctuary of stained glass, music, and congregants, or outdoors surrounded by nature, the trees and animals, and maybe just yourself?

Perhaps Isaac Behunin asked himself that question. An early settler of the spectacular Virgin River valley, Behunin said that we "can worship God among these great cathedrals as well as in any man-made church—this is Zion!" Evoking the Old Testament's paradise sought, captured, then lost by the Jewish nation, he named the place Zion National Park—an earthly paradise.

To lovers of nature and adventure, Zion truly exists in southwestern Utah.

Long ago the Zion area was the world's largest dune field, its sand blown from the Appalachian Mountains. It was transformed into limestone, shale, mudstone, and sandstone, relatively soft rocks that could be carved away by the Virgin River and other streams. What we see now is the most recent work of a river continuing to chisel away at the rock around it, and rain, flash floods, and seeping water eating away at the rock more quietly.

The seasons in Zion

Among the favorite activities for visitors not afraid of getting wet is the hike in the treacherous and exhilarating gorge called The Narrows. The river has cut a narrow slot a thousand feet into the rock, with the gap sometimes just a few dozen feet wide. The Narrows is so tight that no room remains for a trail: you hike in the Virgin River itself. You decide which rock looks stable, how far your legs can stretch, and ultimately where you step. Probably not a trail for the claustrophobic, The Narrows stretches sixteen miles, but even a short venture will give you a great story to share.

While The Narrows lies at the very bottom of the park, the Angels Landing Trail vaults you into the sky, almost 1,500 feet up. Though only five miles round trip, the trail is perhaps the most adventurous, stomach-churning, heart-racing in the National Park System. Atop a sandstone fin jutting into the canyon, the trail is at times extremely narrow and has steep drop-offs on either side. Definitely not a trail for the acrophobic—at some points, chains are all there is between you and the canyon floor—it ends at Angels Landing with a view of the Zion Canyon that will stick with you the rest of your life. Take a deep breath. You'll make it back.

Once you're back on firm ground and your pulse has returned to normal, easier and more moderate trails await. Weeping Rock Trail leads to the eponymous garden, where water has seeped down through Navajo sandstone until it reaches impermeable Kayenta siltstone, which forces it horizontally to the edge of the walls. There, a thousand years after it first rained from the sky, the water drips out and nourishes plants that have adapted to grow in solid rock on the side of a cliff. Flowers, mosses, and ferns live in hanging gardens like this all over the park.

An immensely popular park that attracts more than three million visitors each year, Zion sits at the junction of the Colorado Plateau to the east, the Great Basin to the northwest, and the Mojave Desert to the southwest. With more than a mile's difference in altitude across the park, the resulting blend of ecosystems makes Zion the only home for nine hundred different species.

All around you will be some of God's greatest work: the sculpted rock, bathed in the desert shades of red, rust, cream, brown. The blues of streams and bright greens of the cottonwoods on the banks. The gleam-

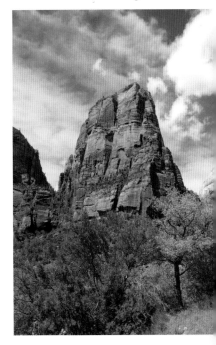

ing white of snow in winter and the forest greens of pines and firs crowning the plateaus will leave you in awe over and over again. Even if you're only taking a short drive through the Zion-Mount Carmel Highway or in the less crowded Kolob Canyons section in the park's northwest quadrant, Zion may inspire heavenly thoughts and visions.

Maybe Isaac Behunin was right.

When you think of paradise, what images or ideas come to mind? How has your perception of paradise changed over the years? How does your idea of paradise compare to others who have different backgrounds, faith stories, or life experiences?

Angels Landing

235

Settling in for the night under the stars of Joshua Tree National Park

BENEDICTION

*A*merica's *Holy Ground* opens with an invocation, calling God into our thoughts and our hearts. Likewise, it closes with a communal blessing.

Consider the lilies of the field, how they grow; they neither toil nor spin, yet I tell you, even Solomon in all his glory was not clothed like one of these.

—MATTHEW 6:28–29 (NRSV)

Nature is full of genius, full of the divinity; so that not a snowflake escapes its fashioning hand.

—HENRY DAVID THOREAU

This grand show is eternal. It is always sunrise somewhere; the dew is never all dried at once; a shower is forever falling; vapor ever rising. Eternal sunrise, eternal sunset, eternal dawn and gloaming, on seas and continents and islands, each in its turn, as the round earth rolls.

—JOHN MUIR

Come forth into the light of things, let nature be your teacher.

—WILLIAM WORDSWORTH

We have the world to live in on the condition that we will take good care of it. And to take good care of it, we have to know it. And to know it and to be willing to take care of it, we have to love it. To cherish what remains of the Earth and to foster its renewal is our only legitimate hope of survival.

—WENDELL BERRY

For the beauty of the earth, for the glory of the skies, for the love which from our birth over and around us lies; Lord of all, to thee we raise this our hymn of grateful praise.

—Folliott Sandford Pierpoint

My country's skies are bluer than the ocean, and sunlight beams on cloverleaf and pine; But other lands have sunlight too, and clover, and skies are everywhere as blue as mine. O hear my song, thou God of all the nations, a song of peace for their land and for mine.

— "Finlandia," lyrics by Veikko Antero Koskenniemi

Life is not measured by the number of breaths you take but by the moments that take your breath away.

—Maya Angelou

Every moment and every event of every man's life on earth plants something in his soul.

—Thomas Merton

We must protect the forests for our children, grandchildren and children yet to be born. We must protect the forests for those who can't speak for themselves such as the birds, animals, fish and trees.

—Chief Qwatsinas (also known as Edward Moody), Nuxalk Nation (Canada)

I hope the United States of America is not so rich that she can afford to let these wildernesses pass by, or so poor she cannot afford to keep them.

—Margaret "Mardy" Murie, conservationist and Alaska National Wildlife Refuge proponent

We have become great because of the lavish use of our resources. . .. But the time
has come to inquire seriously what will happen when our forests are gone, when
the coal, the iron, the oil, and the gas are exhausted, when the soils have been still
further impoverished and washed into the streams, polluting the rivers, denuding
the fields and obstructing navigation.

—THEODORE ROOSEVELT

You can't conserve what you haven't got.

— MARJORY STONEMAN DOUGLAS, AUTHOR, CONSERVATIONIST, AND
EVERGLADES PROPONENT

What a country chooses to save is what a country chooses to say about itself.

—MOLLIE BEATTIE,
DIRECTOR OF THE U.S. FISH AND WILDLIFE SERVICE

Never lose an opportunity to see anything beautiful, for beauty
is God's handwriting.

—RALPH WALDO EMERSON

This is my Father's world and to my listening ears, all nature sings and round me
rings the music of the spheres. This is my Father's world, I rest me in the thought
of rocks and trees, of skies and seas, his hand, the wonders wrought. This is my
Father's world, the birds, their carols raise, the morning light, the lily white
declare their maker's praise. This is my Father's world, he shines in all that's fair.
In the rustling grass I hear Him pass, he speaks to me everywhere. This is my
Father's world, oh let me ne'er forget that though the wrong seems oft so strong,
God is the ruler yet. This is my Father's world; why should my heart be sad? The
Lord is King; let the heavens ring! God reigns; let the earth be glad.

—MALTBIE DAVENPORT BABCOCK

Before the mountains were born
or you brought forth the whole world,
from everlasting to everlasting you are God. . . .
A thousand years in your sight
are like a day that has just gone by,
or like a watch in the night.

—PSALM 90:2, 4 (NIV)

Go for the Grandeur of God's creation.

Go and see the Art of creation all around you.

Go to recall life's Diversity.

Go to see if it's as beautiful in real life as it is in your Imagination.

Go to Return to the site of your favorite dreams, and Remember what it is to marvel.

Go to see nature's Paradox: When circumstances Change, life must Adapt with the unexpected Consequences—and yet nature thrives.

Go because you want to cross Borders, to go to a new Place.

Go because it is Home or it is where your Roots are.

Go because you're on a Mission.

Go for the sake of the Journey or the Experience.

Go because you crave Movement.

Go to celebrate a Beginning, a Landmark, or an Ending.

Go to find Connection, then Reconciliation, then Unity.

Go for the Community and the Companionship and the Teamwork, or go for the Solitude and Isolation.

Go and refresh your Spirit. Go for the Sabbath.

Go for all the Time you need to regain Perspective.

Go and start a new Story.

Go to remember a Language without words.

Go and remember your Name, or forget it for a while.

Go to seek the Turbulence and the Chaos and the Wilderness, and then find Restoration and Emancipation and Joy.

Go in search of Preservation and Protection when Darkness looms.

Go and face Adversity, seek Guidance, remember to Trust, and see the Potential for wondrous things.

Go for Reflection and to see a Vision of what your life could be.

Go to remember the Sustenance and the Foundation of our faith and lives we have in God.

Go and see God Reveal the Signs of divine love all around you.

Go to remember God Nurtures you and expects you in turn to nurture the world we share.

Go and see Paradise, for us to share now and forever.

Go because Life is a Gift from God and we should live every moment as though it is our last.

Go.

And go in Peace. Amen.

Chapel of Transfiguration, Grand Teton National Park

Lower Falls and the Grand Canyon of the Yellowstone River

RESOURCES

The best way to research this book is, of course, to visit each national park and take incredibly detailed notes, photographing every sign, recording every ranger presentation, documenting every nugget from a tourism office worker or hotel front-desk manager or conversations with friends as we show off vacation photos. Unfortunately we were too busy taking in the awe of God's creation to document each and every sign accurately. (Besides, *The Chicago Manual of Style* doesn't detail how to document signage and casual conversations in a bibliography.)

That said, most of our resources will go unnoted here, but what follows are the resources that were most helpful in the researching of this book:

+ *NPS.gov* and its incredibly rich content. Most of the photos in this book are available on NPS.gov and are in the public domain. Thank you to the often-unnamed photographers who produced these breathtaking images. Additionally, we couldn't have done this without NPS.gov's wonderful descriptions, insight, photographs, multimedia, maps, and historical insight.

+ *Park rangers*. Seriously, these folks are brilliant. When you see a park ranger, listen up. You're about to learn something.

+ *Guide to National Parks of the United States (eighth edition)*. National Geographic, Washington, D.C.

+ *Complete National Parks of the United States* by Mel White (Washington, D.C.: National Geographic, 2009).

+ *The 10 Best of Everything: National Parks* by Robert E. Howells, Olivia Garnett, Gary McKetchnie, Jeremy Schmitt, Mel White, and Joe Yogurst (Washington, D.C.: National Geographic, 2011).

- *Wikipedia*'s many pages on national parks and related pages. While not a primary source, Wikipedia was a great way to confirm an accurate memory or correct an inaccurate one.
- *Dear Bob and Sue (One Couple's Journey through the National Parks)* by Matt and Karen Smith. Originally published in 2012, this self-published book has since been revised, and a sequel was published in 2018.

On the Colorado River deep in the Grand Canyon

JOURNAL

_____

_____

_____

_____

_____

_____

_____

_____

_____

_____

Arch at Bryce Canyon

Canyon View lookout, Grand Canyon National Park

Patterns in the sand, Kobuk Valley National Park and Preserve

Sylvan Lake in October, Yellowstone National Park

Newspaper Rock petroglyphs at Petrified Forest National Park

Fire under the stars, Hawai'ian Volcanoes National Park

A single wolf in winter, Isle Royale National Park

Wildflowers, Death Valley National Park

Yosemite Valley Chapel and Upper
Yosemite Fall

PHOTO CREDITS

NPS.gov's extensive photo archive does not always list the photographer, nor does it consistently list whether the photographer was working for the National Park Service when the photo was taken. The credit below reflects how photo credits are (and are not) listed on NPS.gov. Photos by the authors and from Shutterstock are copyrighted. All rights reserved. All other photos are in the public domain.

Regardless of who took the photos and in what capacity they were working, on this we can agree: These photos are holy gifts! Thank you for your work.

PAGE	CREDIT BY	PAGE	CREDIT BY
2	Brad Lyons	58	NPS/Chris Roundtree
5	NPS	59	NPS/Chris Roundtree
6	NPS	60	NPS/Chuck Burton
8-9	Brad Lyons	62	NPS/Peter Jones
10	NPS	63	NPS
13	Brad Lyons	65	NPS
14	Brad Lyons	66	Shuttrstock/wildnerdpix
17	NPS	69	Brad Lyons
18	NPS	70	Brad Lyons
20	Bruce Barkhauer	71	Brad Lyons; NPS
21	Bruce Barkhauer	72	NPS/Jim Schmidt
23	Brad Lyons	74	NPS; NPS
24	NPS/Kristi Rugg	75	NPS; NPS
26	NPS	77	Dianne Milliard
27	NPS	78	NPS
29	NPS	79	Kurt Moses
30	NPS	80	Warren Field
32	NPS/Chris Wonderly	82	NPS
33	NPS/Casey Hodnett	83	Kent Miller; Kent Miller
34	NPS	85	NPS
36	NPS/Cathy Bell	86	NPS
37	NPS/Mackenzie Reed	88	NPS
39	NPS/Jennette Jurado	89	NPS; NPS
40	NPS	91	NPS/Laurie Smith
41	NPS/Ann Wildermuth	92	Brad Lyons
42	NPS	94	NPS
44	NPS/Shaun Wolfe; NPS	95	Brad Lyons
45	NPS	97	NPS/Tim Rains
46	NPS/Victoria Stauffenberg	98	NPS/Jacob W. Frank; NPS
49	Bruce Barkhauer	99	NPS/Jacob W. Frank
50	Bruce Barkhauer	100	NPS/Sean Nielson
52	NPS/Neal Herbert	102	NPS
54	NPS/Neal Herbert	103	NPS
55	NPS	104	Bruce Barkhauer
57	NPS/Jacob Frank	106	Bruce Barkhauer

PAGE	CREDIT BY	PAGE	CREDIT BY
107	Bruce Barkhauer; Bruce Barkhauer	182	Bruce Barkhauer
		183	Bruce Barkhauer
109	Brad Lyons	184	NPS
110	NPS; D. Lehle	186	NPS/Kurt Moses
111	D. Lehle	187	NPS/Rebecca Ouvry
112	NPS	189	NPS
115	NPS/Patrick Myers	190	NPS
116	NPS	191	NPS
117	NPS	192	Jon Olsen
118	Brad Lyons	194	NPS
120	NPS; Bruce Barkhauer	195	NPS
121	NPS	197	Bruce Barkhauer
123	D. Buehler	198	Bruce Barkhauer
124	Polly Angelakis	199	Bruce Barkhauer
126	Elizabeth Havelin	201	Brad Lyons
127	Wendy Swee/NPS J.Frost	202	Brad Lyons
129	NPS/S. Geiger	204	NPS/Neal Lewis
130	NPS	206	Brad Lyons
131	Bruce Barkhauer	207	NPS/Neal Lewis
132	Brad Lyons	209	NPS/Boyd Turner
134	Brad Lyons	211	NPS/Rolan Honeyman
135	Brad Lyons; NPS	212	Anne Finney
136	J. Crocker	214	Susanna Pershern
139	Lindsey Welch	215	Kimberly Boulon
140	NPS/Brad Sutton	217	NPS
142	Brad Lyons; NPS/Kurt Moses	218	Shutterstock/Zack Frank
143	NPS/Larry McAfee	220	NPS
145	NPS	221	NPS
146	NPS	223	NPS/Neal Herbert
148	NPS	224	Brad Lyons
149	NPS/Jim Pfeiffenberger	227	NPS/Jim Peaco
151	Brad Lyons	229	NPS/James Miller
152	D. Malengo	230	NPS
153	Scott Toste	231	Shutterstock; Sebastien Gabriel
155	NPS		
157	NPS/Kevyn Jalone	232	NPS
158	Brad Lyons	234	NPS; NPS/Amy Gaiennie
161	NPS	235	NPS
163	Shutterstock/rukawajung	236	NPS/Hannah Schwalbe
164	NPS	241	NPS
165	NPS	242	Brad Lyons
166	NPS	244	NPS/Mark Lellouch
169	NPS/Sandy Groves	245	Bruce Barkhauer
171	NPS	246-247	Bruce Barkhauer
172	NPS	248	NPS
173	NPS/Emily Brouwer; NPS/Steven Redman	249	Brad Lyons
		250	Bruce Barkhauer
175	NPS/Keith Brumund-Smith	251	NPS/S. Geiger
176	Bruce Barkhauer	252	Rolf Peterson
178	Bruce Barkhauer; NPS	253	NPS/Emily McCuistion
179	Bruce Barkhauer	254	Brad Lyons
181	Bruce Barkhauer		